Sports in America
1990–1999

SECOND EDITION

Bob Woods

SERIES FOREWORD BY
LARRY KEITH

CHELSEA HOUSE
PUBLISHERS
An imprint of Infobase Publishing

1990–1999, Second Edition
Sports in America

Copyright © 2010, 2004 Bob Woods
Foreword copyright © 2010 Larry Keith

Chelsea House
An imprint of Infobase Publishing
132 West 31st Street
New York NY 10001

Library of Congress Cataloging-in-Publication Data

Woods, Bob.
 Sports in America, 1990-1999 / Bob Woods ; series foreword by Larry Keith. — 2nd ed.
   p. cm. — (Sports in America)
 Includes bibliographical references and index.
 ISBN-13: 978-1-60413-456-8 (hardcover : alk. paper)
 ISBN-10: 1-60413-456-9 (hardcover : alk. paper) 1. Sports—United States—History—20th century. I. Title. II. Series.

 GV583.W66 2010
 796.097309′049—dc22

                    2010011083

Chelsea House books are available at special discounts when purchased in bulk quantities for businesses, associations, institutions, or sales promotions. Please call our Special Sales Department in New York at (212) 967-8800 or (800) 322-8755.

You can find Chelsea House on the World Wide Web at http://www.chelseahouse.com

Produced by the Shoreline Publishing Group LLC
President/Editorial Director: James Buckley Jr.
Contributing Editors: Jim Gigliotti, Beth Adelman
Text design by Thomas Carling, carlingdesign.com
Index by Nanette Cardon, IRIS

Photo credits: AP/Wide World: 3, 8, 9, 11, 21, 23, 29, 32, 33, 36, 37, 39, 41, 43, 47, 48, 49, 52, 54, 55, 56, 59, 64, 65, 71, 73, 75, 76, 78, 81, 83, 84, 88, 89; Corbis: 7, 25, 62, 68; Getty Images: 14, 15, 17, 19, 24, 27, 30, 35, 51, 67. Sports icons by Bob Eckstein.

Cover printed by Bang Printing, Brainerd, MN
Book printed and bound by Bang Printing, Brainerd, MN
Date printed: July 2010

Printed in the United States of America.

10 9 8 7 6 5 4 3 2 1

This book is printed on acid-free paper.

CONTENTS

Sheryl Swoopes (page 36)

FOREWORD

BY LARRY KEITH

WHEN THE EDITORS OF SPORTS IN AMERICA invited me to write the foreword to this important historical series I recalled my experience in the 1980s as the adjunct professor for a new sports journalism course in the graduate school of Columbia University. Before granting their approval, the faculty at that prestigious Ivy League institution asked, Do sports matter? Are they relevant? Are they more than just fun and games?

The answer—an emphatic yes—is even more appropriate today than it was then. As an integral part of American society, sports provide insights to our history and culture and, for better or worse, help define who we are.

Sports In America is much more than a compilation of names, dates, and facts. Each volume chronicles accomplishments and expansions of the possible. Not just in the physical ability to perform, but in the ability to create goals and determine methods to achieve them. In this way, sports, the sweaty offspring of recreation and competition, resemble any other field of endeavor. I certainly wouldn't equate the race for a gold medal with the race to the moon, but the building blocks are the same: the intelligent application of talent, determination, research, practice, and hard work to a meaningful objective.

Sports matter because they show us in high definition. They communicate examples of determination, courage, and skill. They often embody a heroic human-interest story, overcoming poverty, injustice, injury, or disease. The phrase, "Sports is a microcosm of life," could also read "Life is a microcosm of sport."

Consider racial issues. When Jackie Robinson of the Brooklyn Dodgers broke through major league baseball's "color barrier" in 1947, the significance extended beyond the national pastime. Precisely because baseball was the national pastime, this epochal event reverberated throughout every part of American society.

To be sure, black stars from individual sports had preceded him (notably Joe Louis in boxing and Jesse Owens in track), and others would follow (Arthur Ashe in tennis and Tiger Woods in golf), but Robinson stood out as an important member of a team. He wasn't just playing with the Dodgers, he was traveling with them, living with them. He was a black member of a white athletic family. The benefits of integration could be appreciated far beyond the borough of Brooklyn. In 1997, Major League Baseball retired his "42" jersey number.

Sports have always been a laboratory for social awareness and change. Robinson integrated big league box scores eight years before the U.S. Supreme Court ordered the integration of public schools. The Paralympics (1960) and Special Olympics (1968) easily predate the Americans with Disabilities Act (1990). The mainstreaming of disabled athletes was especially apparent in 2007 when double amputee Jessica Long, 15, won the AAU Sullivan Award as America's top amateur. Women's official debut in the Olympic Games, though limited to swimming, occurred in 1912, seven years before they got the right to vote. So even if these sports were tardy in opening their doors, in another way, they were ahead of their times. And if it was necessary to break down some of those doors—Title IX support for female college athletes comes to mind—so be it. Basketball star Candace Parker won't let anyone keep her from the hoop.

Another area of importance, particularly as it affects young people, is substance abuse. High school, college, and professional teams all oppose the illegal use of drugs, tobacco, and alcohol. In most venues, testing is mandatory, and tolerance is zero. The confirmed use of performance enhancing drugs has damaged the reputations of such superstar athletes as Olympic sprinters Ben Johnson and Marion Jones, cyclist Floyd Landis, and baseball sluggers Manny Ramirez and Alex Rodriguez. Some athletes have lost their careers, or even their lives, to substance abuse. Conversely, other athletes have used their fame to caution young people about submitting to peer pressure or making poor choices.

Fans care about sports and sports personalities because they provide entertainment and self-identify—too often at a loss of priorities. One reason sports have flourished in this country is their support from governmental bodies. When a city council votes to help underwrite the cost of a sports facility or give financial advantages to the owners of a team, it affects the pocketbook of every taxpayer, not to mention the local ecosystem. When high schools and colleges allocate significant resources to athletics, administrators believe they are serving the greater good, but at what cost? Decisions with implications beyond the sports page merit everyone's attention.

In World War II, our country's sporting passion inspired President Franklin Roosevelt to declare that professional games should not be cancelled. He felt the benefits to the national psyche outweighed the risk of gathering large crowds at central locations. In 2001, another generation of Americans also continued to attend large-scale sports events because, to do otherwise, would "let the terrorists win." Being there, being a fan, yelling your lungs out, cheering victory and bemoaning defeat, is a cleansing, even therapeutic exercise. The security check at the gate is just part of the price of stepping inside. Even before there was a 9/11, there was a bloody terrorist assault at the Munich Olympic Games in 1972.

The popular notion "Sports build character" has been better expressed "Sports reveal character." We've witnessed too many coaches and athletes break rules of fair play and good conduct. The convictions of NBA referee Tim Donaghy for gambling and NFL quarterback Michael Vick for operating a dog-fighting ring are startling recent examples. We've even seen violence and cheating in youth sports, often by parents of a (supposed) future superstar. We've watched (at a safe distance) fans "celebrate" championships with destructive behavior. I would argue, however, that these flaws are the exception, not the rule, that the good of sports far outweighs the bad, that many of life's success stories took root on an athletic field.

Any serious examination of sports leads to the question of athletes as standards for conduct. Professional basketball star Charles Barkley created quite a stir in 1993 when he used a Nike shoe commercial to declare, "I am not paid to be a role model." The knee-jerk response argued, "Of course you are, because kids look up to you," but Barkley was right to raise the issue. He was saying that, in making lifestyle choices in language and behavior, young people should look elsewhere for role models, ideally to responsible parents or guardians.

The fact remains, however, that athletes occupy an exalted place in our society, especially when they are magnified in the mass media, sports talk radio, and the blogosphere. The athletes we venerate can be as young as a high school basketball player or as old as a Hall of Famer. (They can even be dead, as Babe Ruth's commercial longevity attests.) They are honored and coddled in a way few mortals are. Regrettably, we can be quick to excuse their excesses and ignore their indulgences. They influence the way we live and think: Ted Williams inspired patriotism as a wartime fighter pilot; Muhammad Ali's opposition to the Vietnam War on religious grounds, validated by the Supreme Court, encouraged the peace movement; Magic Johnson's contraction of the HIV/AIDs virus brought better understanding to a little-understood disease. No wonder we elect them—track stars, football coaches, baseball pitchers—to represent us in Washington. Meanwhile, television networks pay huge sums to sports leagues so their teams can pay fortunes for their services.

Indeed, it has always been this way. If we, as a nation, love sports, then we, quite naturally, will love the men and women who play them best. In return, they provide entertainment, release and inspiration. From the beginning of the 20th century until now, Sports In America is their story-and ours.

Larry Keith is the former Assistant Managing Editor of Sports Illustrated. *He created the editorial concept for* SI Kids *and was the editor of the official Olympic programs in 1996, 2000 and 2002. He is a former adjunct professor of Sports Journalism at Columbia University and is a member of the North Carolina Journalism Hall of Fame.*

INTRODUCTION
1990–1999

The 1990s was the decade of the Internet revolution, a time when sports and their stars were brought into everyone's homes instantaneously by the wonders of high-speed technology. No longer did sports fans have to wait for the morning paper to see the box scores or read about their favorite teams. They were at their fingertips along the information superhighway at the click of a button (or a mouse).

But even as America hurtled into the digital age, there were nostalgic efforts to cling to the past, such as baseball's new "retro" ballparks that called to mind the fields of earlier years, and the revival of bell-bottom pants in the fashion world.

America enjoyed a period of relative peace and prosperity during the final decade of the 20th century. Alarming news of AIDS, terrorism, and homelessness was often drowned out by the sirens of pop celebrity. Even the Persian Gulf War of 1991 generated an uplifting spin. It was especially evident at the star-spangled Super Bowl XXV in Tampa, Florida, where patriotism packed more punch than the Buffalo Bills' offense.

The first President George Bush couldn't win the battle against economic woes, however, and the nation moved into eight colorful, if controversial, years under Bill Clinton. About the same time that Wall Street's bulls started running wild and the economy skyrocketed, spurred by high-flying dotcom stocks, Chicago's Bulls, behind the gravity-defying feats of Michael Jordan, won the first of their six National Basketball Association (NBA) titles in the 1990s. Reflecting the go-go decade, Air Jordan was equally admired for his commercial endorsements, hugely popular sneaker brand, and ranking atop *Forbes Magazine's* list of richest athletes.

The rite of calling sports a selfish business and referring to athletes as pampered brats dates back to ancient times, when Greek senators cried foul over paying "amateur" Olympians and shut down the original Games because of corruption. In the 1990s, however, the volume of complaints went way up. Free agency, which enabled players to sign with any team, left fans rooting for uniforms rather than the millionaire players in them. The cliché "the best team money can buy" was put to work by George Steinbrenner, Wayne Huizenga, Daniel Snyder, and other wealthy owners. Kids bounded straight from high school to the NBA,

A Windows World *CEO Bill Gates and the Microsoft Corporation were at the forefront of the digital age.*

and underclassmen left college in droves for the National Football League (NFL). And, incredibly—for the first time since 1904—the World Series was cancelled in 1994 because striking players couldn't agree with stubborn owners on how to divvy up billions of dollars.

The thud of sports heroes falling grew louder, too. O.J. Simpson ran from the law instead of tacklers and Mike Tyson raged

1990–1999

inside a jail cell rather than a boxing ring, reminding us just how fragile are our anointed champions. We may have wagged our fingers, but still, we couldn't turn away. Scandal fed the public's appetite for controversy and the media's rush to cover it. The decade witnessed everything from President Clinton versus Monica Lewinsky to Nancy Kerrigan versus Tonya Harding (see page 45).

In the process, television's reach expanded exponentially. Along with 24-hour general news, sports, weather, and entertainment, cable TV carved such niches as The Golf Channel, SpeedVision, and Court TV. The networks fought tooth and nail for the chance to shell out obscene amounts of money for the broadcast rights to sporting events, regardless of the fact that viewership numbers kept dropping. To pay those bills, and the sports announcers' gigantic salaries, they sold sponsorships to kickoffs, halftime shows, pitching changes, and anything else that could feature a corporate logo.

While cynicism, shame, and greed ran rampant throughout the 1990s, sports fans did have plenty to honestly cheer about. Among the highlights: Bonnie Blair's five Olympic gold medals in speed skating, Cal Ripken Jr.'s streak of consecutive baseball games played, Greg LeMond's three-peat in the Tour de France bicycle race, John Elway's back-to-back Super Bowl wins, Christian Laettner's miraculous basketball shot on the way to the college championship, Dale Earnhardt's first Daytona 500 victory, the New York Rangers' Stanley Cup win to snap a 53-year drought, sprinter Michael Johnson's unprecedented Olympic double, Tiger Woods' obliteration of the Augusta golf course, and Mark McGwire's 70th home run.

Sports and society connected in other ways in the decade. Though American society as a whole had come a long way in addressing racial inequities by 1990, lingering issues gained attention via the sports world. Shoal Creek Country Club's admission of its first African-American

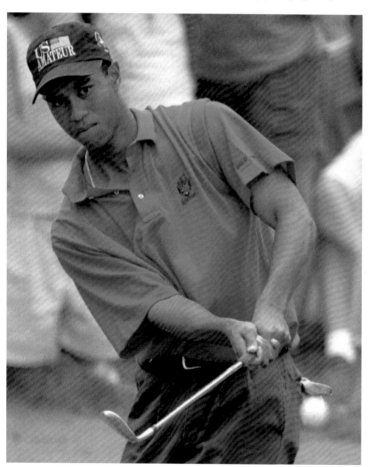

Eye of the Tiger *Tiger Woods eyes a chip during his unprecedented third consecutive United States Amateur championship in 1996. Woods soon took the men's pro golf tour by storm, too.*

member that year—only under extreme pressure—and the fuss over Woods' arrival on the pro golf scene in 1996 only magnified how much the game of golf remained starkly white. On the other hand, just as the O.J. Simpson trial exposed a rift between blacks and whites, baseball's celebration of the 50th anniversary of Jackie Robinson's major league debut provided some healing.

Women overwhelmingly proved their place in sports during the 1990s. Increased opportunities and funding for women's high school and college sports programs, federally mandated by Title IX in 1975, reaped rewards with Olympic championships in soccer, volleyball, and softball. The U.S. soccer team won two of the first three World Cups for women, including a thrilling tournament on American turf in 1999. And women's basketball hit the big time, exemplified by outstanding college teams at the University of Connecticut and the University of Tennessee, where individuals such as Rebecca Lobo and Chamique Holdsclaw gained superstar status. Women literally "got game" when the NBA spun off the Women's National Basketball Association in 1997.

As the country headed into the uncharted waters of the 21st century, it could turn, as past generations always have, to sports and athletes for inspiration. "The spirit, the will to win, and the will to excel are the things that endure," said Vince Lombardi, the late, great football coach and motivator. "These qualities are so much more important than the events that occur."

That indomitable spirit came shining through when one-handed baseball

Women Go Pro   *The continuing rise of women in sports was signaled with the debut of the Women's National Basketball Association in 1997. Nykesha Sales of the Connecticut Sun was one of several players who gained national stardom.*

pitcher Jim Abbott threw a no-hitter, when speed skater Dan Jansen picked himself up until he won a gold medal, and when cancer survivor Lance Armstrong captured cycling's grueling Tour de France. Their courage and perseverance gave everyone hope that greatness can still be achieved.

1990

Bo Knows Rose Bowl Woes

The University of Southern California (USC) Trojans spoiled the final game of University of Michigan Wolverines coach Glenn "Bo" Schembechler's (1929–2006) career with a 17–10 victory in the Rose Bowl on January 1 in Pasadena, California.

Schembechler coached for 27 seasons at the University of Miami in Ohio (from 1963 to 1968) and at Michigan (1969 to 1989). He compiled a stellar overall record of 234–65–8 and led his teams to 15 conference championships, including 13 Big Ten crowns while at Michigan. But if he had one blip on his résumé, it was a 5–12 record in bowl games, including a 2–8 mark in the Rose Bowl.

Michigan believed it could send Schembechler out on a high note, though, when it took a 10–1 team into Pasadena to face the 8–2–1 Trojans, the champions of the Pacific-10 Conference.

This USC squad featured rookie sensation quarterback Todd Marinovich. His 22-of-31 passing performance, coupled with Pasadena-born running back Ricky Ervins' 126 rushing yards, eventually overcame a valiant Michigan effort.

With 12 minutes remaining in the game, the score was tied at 10–10. Michigan's defense had held USC to 27 third-quarter yards, and now the offense had the ball on its own 46-yard line, with momentum seemingly on Schembechler's side. There was a growing sense among the sold-out crowd of 103,450 that the Wolverines might soon be carrying their coach off the field on their victorious shoulders and into a glorious sunset.

Just like that, though, a holding penalty on a fake punt play nullified a would-be first down for the Wolverines. Michigan was forced to punt—for real. The Trojans chewed up yardage and the clock on their next possession. They marched 75 yards in 13 plays, culminated with a 14-yard, game-winning touchdown run by Ervins with 1:10 left.

Even in his eighth Rose Bowl defeat, Schembechler made the final walk off the football field with his head held high. The Wolverines had their first 10-win season since 1986 and earned their second consecutive outright Big Ten championship. After 21 seasons in Ann Arbor, Schembechler retired as the winningest coach in Michigan football history, with a 194–48–5 record. He went out a winner.

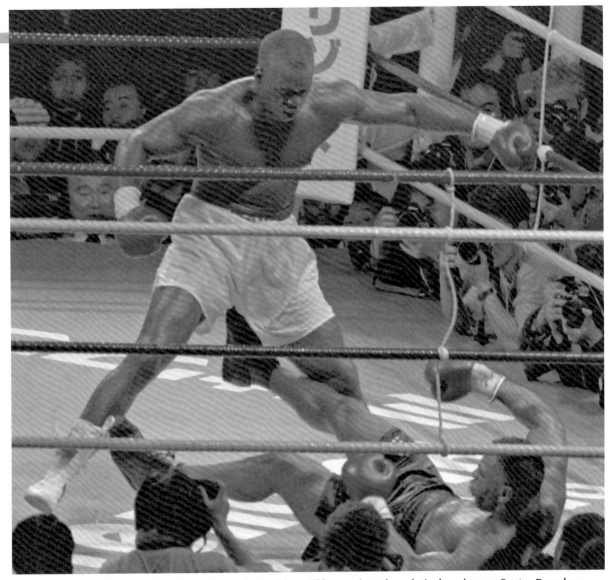

Buster Who? *Mike Tyson (on the mat) was invincible until he ran into the relatively unknown Buster Douglas.*

The Fall of Tyson, Part I

Few people outside the boxing world had ever heard of James "Buster" Douglas (b.1960) before February 11. And even those familiar with the sport didn't give the 6-foot-4, 230-pound fighter much of a chance against heavyweight champion Mike Tyson (b.1966). After all, the ferocious "Iron Mike" was undefeated in 37 bouts, winning 33 by knockouts. His opponents were lucky to last beyond the first round. So when Douglas stepped into the ring that night in Tokyo, Japan, it was no surprise that he was a 42–1 underdog. The surprise came a bit later.

Media Milestones

✔ On January 31, *The National Sports Daily*, America's first all-sports newspaper, made its debut in New York, Chicago, and Los Angeles. Edited by Frank Deford, it folded in 18 months.

✔ NBC did not stand for Notre Dame Broadcasting Company, even though the network signed a five-year, $30-million deal to broadcast 30 University of Notre Dame home football games from 1991 to 1995.

✔ In March, CBS renewed its NFL contract, paying more than $1 billion to telecast National Football Conference (NFC) games for four more years, as well as the 1992 Super Bowl. A day later, NBC paid $752 million for four more years of American Football Conference (AFC) games and the 1993 Super Bowl.

✔ On April Fool's Day, CBS fired broadcaster Brent Musburger after 15 years with the network, but did allow him to broadcast the National Collegiate Athletic Association (NCAA) men's basketball championship game the next day. A month later, he signed a six-year deal with ABC Sports.

✔ Al Michaels became the highest-paid television sportscaster by signing a five-year contract with ABC for $2.5 million a year.

✔ In October, the long-time radio play-by-play broadcaster for basketball's Boston Celtics, Johnny Most, retired at the age of 67.

Early on, it became apparent that this fight would not be another typical Tyson demolition job. The much bigger Douglas used his incredible 13-inch reach advantage and lightning jab effectively to stun the 5-foot-11 Tyson. A punishing right wobbled Iron Mike in the fifth round and raised a welt over his left eye. The champ grew increasingly frustrated. Still, he battled back, and late in the eighth round he caught Douglas with a vicious uppercut that dropped the challenger to the canvas. Douglas barely recovered, rising at the count of nine.

The 10th round will go down in history as one of boxing's most memorable. With a relentless combination of punches, Douglas sent Tyson tumbling down. The champ stumbled to his feet, but was clearly dazed. The referee stopped the fight and declared Douglas the winner and new champion. Boxing commentator Larry Merchant said afterward, "The Japanese people came to see Godzilla, only the wrong person turned out to be Godzilla." It remains one of the greatest upsets in sports history—even more so considering that Douglas' unexpected reign ended just eight and a half months later, when he lost his only title defense to Evander Holyfield.

Terrific Twins of Lacrosse

The Gait brothers—identical twins Gary and Paul (b.1967)—carried the undefeated Syracuse University men's lacrosse team to its third consecutive NCAA championship with a 21–9 victory over Loyola (Maryland) on May 28. (The title later was vacated because of NCAA rules violations.)

The tandem talents of the Gait twins, seniors on the Orange lacrosse squad, produced one of the most dynamic duos in collegiate sports history. In that lopsided championship contest—both the goal total and margin of victory set NCAA finals records—they scored eight goals and finished their four-year careers with a combined 319 goals and 146 assists. In the three games Syracuse played in the 1990 postseason, Gary's nine goals established the record for the most ever scored in the NCAA tournament. He also owns another NCAA record for the most goals scored in a single game (nine), in a May 1988 shellacking of Navy.

The Gaits' stick handling, passing, shooting, and overall athleticism dazzled fans and befuddled opponents with moves that had never been seen before. In one, a lacrosse version of basketball's alley-oop play, Paul would lob a high pass to Gary as he streaked across the front of the goal. Gary cradled the ball above his head, and while still airborne and with his back to the mouth of the goal, he would bring his stick down and whip the ball between his legs and into the net.

More spectacular was Gary's jaw-dropping "Air Gait" play, first witnessed during an NCAA championship semifinal match in 1988 against the University of Pennsylvania. Cradling the ball behind the Penn goal and just outside the protective crease, Gary leapt toward the front of the net. He flew over the goal, angled his stick in front of it, and, using the crossbar as a fulcrum, jammed the ball into the net—the equivalent of lacrosse's first slam dunk. (This move is no longer legal.)

Invented centuries ago by Native Americans, lacrosse has a storied history at Syracuse. Jim Brown (b.1936), who played football at Syracuse and later for the Cleveland Browns, also starred on the university's lacrosse team (as well as its track and basketball teams) in the mid-1950s. He is still regarded as one of the best collegiate lacrosse players ever. Since 1971, when the NCAA added lacrosse to its roster of sanctioned sports, Syracuse has won eight championships. A true

dynasty, the Orangemen advanced to the final game every year from 1983 to 2002.

The brothers Gait went on to record-setting careers in professional lacrosse, and remain instrumental in promoting the sport in youth and high school programs.

In the same induction class (of course!) in 2005, both brothers were enshrined in the United States Lacrosse National Hall of Fame.

The Bad Boys Are Good

The Detroit Pistons had finally reached the NBA mountaintop in 1989, winning a championship for the first time in the franchise's 41-year history. Yet critics wondered if their four-game sweep of the Los Angeles Lakers in the best-of-seven-games NBA Finals had more to do with hamstring injuries to L.A.'s Earvin "Magic" Johnson (b.1959) and Byron Scott than a truly outstanding Pistons team. Were they merely a one-year wonder?

The Pistons silenced the critics with a hard-fought defense of their championship in June, beating the Portland Trail Blazers, four games to one. In the process, Detroit joined the Lakers and Boston Celtics as the only teams in NBA history to win consecutive titles.

The 1989–1990 Pistons reflected the tough, hard-working personality of the Motor City. Head coach Chuck Daly (1930–2009) preached defense, and his players heeded his words well—sometimes too well, other teams charged. With an aggressive, hard-fouling, in-your-face style, they became known as the NBA's Bad Boys.

1990

Call them what you will, the Pistons had the league's stingiest defense, holding opponents to 98.3 points per game and a .447 shooting percentage.

Daly made up for the off-season loss of power forward and chief enforcer Rick Mahorn to the expansion Minnesota Timberwolves by moving James Edwards and Dennis Rodman (b.1961) into the starting rotation opposite bruising center Bill Laimbeer. All-star point guard Isiah Thomas (b.1961), Joe Dumars, and Vin-

nie "the Microwave" Johnson propelled a lethal outside shooting game. Detroit finished the season with an Eastern Conference-best record of 59–23, highlighted by a 25–1 streak running from January to March.

The Trail Blazers pulled into suburban Detroit's Palace of Auburn Hills for game one of the finals with an identical won-lost record. Led by high-flying scoring machine Clyde Drexler (averaging 23.3 points per game, point guard Terry Porter, and power forward Buck Williams, Portland wasn't about to roll over for the Bad Boys. In fact, their intensity on both ends of the court caught the Pistons by surprise for three quarters, and the Trailblazers led, 90–80, with seven minutes left in the game.

That's the point at which Thomas took over. His offensive outburst, featuring a seven-point barrage, inspired the defense, which made huge stops and forced turnovers. A pair of Thomas three-point baskets sparked a come-from-behind, 105–99 victory.

Game two in Detroit turned into another tight affair. Despite an inspired second-half effort by Laimbeer—he scored 19 points in the last 17 minutes—the game went into overtime. With four seconds left in overtime, Laimbeer hit the last of his six three-pointers, tying an NBA Finals record, to put the Pistons up by one. But Drexler was fouled by Rodman with two seconds remaining and coolly swished both free throws. The Trailblazers escaped with a 106–105 win, taking away Detroit's home-court advantage and sending the series to Portland's Memorial Coliseum for the next three games.

Point Man   *Point guard Isiah Thomas (left) was the man who made the Pistons go. He earned MVP honors in Detroit's five-game victory over Portland in the NBA Finals.*

The Pistons hadn't won a game at the Portland Coliseum in 17 years, and they were without the services of NBA Defensive Player of the Year Rodman, who was out with an ankle injury. Those obstacles didn't seem to matter as Detroit's offense caught fire. No one was hotter than Dumars, who scored 33 points. The Microwave sizzled with 21 points, and the home team got smoked, 121–106.

Both teams ran hot and cold in game four. Portland raced to a 32–22 first-quarter lead, but scored only 14 points in the second period and was down 51–46 at the half. Thomas poured in 22 points in the third period, then the Trailblazers countered with a 28–11 run to take a 93–92 lead with 5:20 left in the game. A see-saw battle ensued down the stretch, until the Pistons were up by three points with 1.8 seconds on the clock. A 35-foot shot by Portland's Danny Young went in, but the referees concluded that time had run out before he took the shot.

Portland, trying to become the first NBA team to come back from a 3–1 deficit in the finals, led by eight points with 10 minutes to play in game five. Johnson heated up again, however, scoring 16 points and lifting Detroit to a 90–90 tie in the final seconds. To cap off his scintillating performance, the Microwave sank a 15-footer with 0:00.7 showing on the clock. Portland's goose was officially cooked. The Pistons won, 92–90.

Despite his teammates' heroics, Thomas received the series' Most Valuable Player trophy. Along with sinking 11 of 16 shots from three-point range, he averaged 27.6 points, eight assists, and 5.2 rebounds in the five games.

Like Father, Like Son

Young Ken Griffey Jr. grew up hanging around Riverfront Stadium in Cincinnati, watching the "Big Red Machine" of the Cincinnati Reds dominate baseball for much of the 1970s.

Griffey's dad, Ken Griffey Sr. was a key player on those Reds teams. An outfielder, he was a three-time All-Star who batted a career-best .336 for the Reds' 1976 champs.

Griffey Jr. idolized his dad, and dreamed of becoming a big-leaguer himself, but at six years old in 1975, he never could have foreseen playing in the same outfield with him.

In 1989, though, the younger Griffey made it to the Majors at age 19 with the Seattle Mariners, the team that selected him with the top overall pick of the 1987 amateur draft. In 1990, the elder Griffey signed with Seattle as a free agent on August 29. Two days later, the Griffeys became the first father-and-son combination ever to take the field together when they were in the Mariners' outfield against the Kansas City Royals.

Two weeks later, the elder Griffey homered in the first inning off starter Kirk McCaskill of the Angels. After greeting his dad at home plate, the younger Griffey stepped into the batter's box and hit a home run himself.

1990

Course of a Different Color

Slavery ended in the United States in 1862, yet it took more than 100 years for Congress to pass the Civil Rights Act of 1964, outlawing discrimination based on race, color, religion, or national origin.

It took another 26 years for Shoal Creek Country Club in Birmingham, Alabama, to grant membership to an African American. And that came about only after Shoal Creek's policy of no black members was exposed shortly before the club was set to host the Professional Golfers' Association (PGA) 1990 Championship. The policy sparked a nationwide controversy and forced the change.

Birmingham had been the center of racial upheaval in 1963, when police attacked civil rights demonstrators with dogs and fire hoses. And while race relations in the United States had greatly improved by 1990 in many areas—including education, employment, and business opportunities—private golf clubs throughout the country remained largely whites-only bastions. Many didn't permit women, Jews, Hispanics, or other minorities to join, either. Such exclusionary rules were seldom challenged or even publicized—until Shoal Creek.

In late June, two months before the PGA Championship, the *Birmingham Post-Herald* ran a story about Shoal Creek. Quoted in the article, its founder, Hall Thompson, stated flatly, "This country club is our home and we pick and choose whom we want. . . . I think we've said that we don't discriminate in every other area except the blacks." Thompson apologized later for his remarks, but he didn't retract them.

Overnight, outrage and protest erupted. The word quickly spread, too, that Shoal Creek was hardly alone. Of the 39 PGA Tour events in 1990, at least 17 had been or were to be held at clubs with no black members, the *Charlotte Observer* reported. The United States Golf Association (USGA), which runs the U.S. Open, had scheduled four of the next five Opens at all-white clubs. Suddenly, the golf establishment's dirty laundry was hung out for all to see.

Protests demanding that the PGA move the tournament to another site went unheeded at first, as did calls for Shoal Creek to drop its racist policy. There was only one black professional golfer on the Tour then, so there wasn't much dissent from the players' ranks. That all changed, however, when IBM, Toyota, Sharp Electronics, and other advertisers threatened to pull out of the PGA Championship broadcast on ABC and ESPN. Before long, Shoal Creek admitted its first black member, and the PGA Tour announced that it would no longer hold tournaments at clubs that discriminate. Similar standards were soon adopted by the USGA and the Ladies Professional Golf Association (LPGA).

The actual tournament in August, nearly a footnote amid the turmoil, eventually was won by Wayne Grady. The Australian shot a four-round total of 282 and edged American Fred Couples by three strokes; Couples bogeyed (shot one over par) four straight holes on the last nine holes of the course to see his championship hopes slip away.

Other Milestones of 1990

✔ Super Bowl XXIV on January 28 was a super blowout, as the San Francisco 49ers corralled the Denver Broncos 55–10. The 49ers set a host of records in the game, including most points and largest margin of victory. Quarterback Joe Montana passed for a record five touchdowns (since broken by San Francisco's Steve Young) and became the first, and still only, player to be named the Super Bowl's Most Valuable Player three times.

✔ Major League Baseball owners locked out players from spring training for 32 days in March and April, delaying the start of the regular season by one week.

✔ Loyola Marymount University's All-America basketball forward Hank Gathers died of heart failure after collapsing on the court during a West Coast Conference tournament game on March 7.

✔ In her professional debut in March, 13-year-old Jennifer Capriati reached the finals of the Virginia Slims tennis tournament.

✔ The University of Wisconsin's Suzy Favor won the 800-meter and 1,500-meter races at the NCAA Track and Field Championships in March, giving her nine individual titles and making her the winningest athlete in NCAA history.

Suzy Favor

✔ In the most lopsided victory ever in an NCAA men's basketball championship game, the University of Nevada-Las Vegas whipped Duke University on April 2, 103–73.

✔ Oakland A's outfielder Jose Canseco signed a new contract that made him the first baseball player to earn more than $5 million a year.

✔ On June 10, 16-year-old Monica Seles became the youngest player ever to win tennis' French Open. It was the first of her nine career Grand Slam singles titles.

✔ On July 24, baseball's all-time hits leader, Pete Rose, was sentenced to federal prison for five months and fined $50,000 for income tax evasion.

Little Leaguers of the Far East

Baseball may be America's pastime, but don't tell that to Little Leaguers in Taiwan. In Williamsport, Pennsylvania, where the sport's truly world series is played annually among teams from around the globe, the 1990 Little League Championship was won by Taiwan, which shut out the team from Shippensburg, Pennsylvania, 9–0, in the August final.

The win was no fluke, either. Taiwan obliterated its three opponents in the tournament by a combined tally of 43–1. The championship was Taiwan's 14th in the last 22 years. "The game of baseball is very beautiful," said manager Wang Tzyy-Tsann. "You can play it to perfection if you pay attention to the fundamentals."

1991

Wide Right

Super Bowl XXV will forever be summed up by two words: wide right. But depending on whether you're a fan of the New York Giants or the Buffalo Bills, they're famous or infamous. Hearing them will make you either stand up and cheer or break down and cry.

On January 27, with eight seconds left in the closest Super Bowl ever played, the Giants led, 20–19. Bills kicker Scott Norwood, with the ball on New York's 47-yard line, trotted onto the field to attempt a game-winning field goal. Adam Lingner snapped the ball and holder Frank Reich placed it cleanly on the grass. Norwood ran up to it, swung his right leg, and the ball sailed toward the goal posts. As players on both sidelines watched (or couldn't) and prayed (that God really does take sides in sports events), the ball strayed to the right. It wound up wide by several feet. The game was over; the Giants had won. The thrill of victory, the agony of defeat.

This agony-and-ecstasy ending was only fitting, considering the stark contrast between the Giants and the Bills when they arrived at Tampa Stadium in Tampa, Florida, on what was already unlike any previous Super Sunday. The United States was at war with Iraq (see the box on this page), and security at the stadium was extraordinary. So was the outpouring of patriotism among the 73,813 in attendance: American flags waving, chants of "U-S-A" reverberating, fighter jets overhead flying, Whitney Houston's inspiring rendition of the national anthem.

The Giants advanced to the NFL championship game on the strength of their defense, which was the best in the league during the regular season. It would need to be near perfect to counter the NFL's highest-scoring offense, the Bills. New York had given up a total of just 16

The Persian Gulf War

On January 16, Operation Desert Storm went into action in the Middle East. Responding to the surprise invasion of Kuwait by neighboring Iraq and its dictator, Saddam Hussein, on August 2, 1990, an American-led coalition of nations launched a massive air attack aimed at destroying Iraq's military. On February 24, the coalition's ground forces entered Kuwait and southern Iraq. After four intense days of fighting, Iraq was defeated and Kuwait was liberated. There had been some talk of canceling the Super Bowl, but the NFL decided the game should go on.

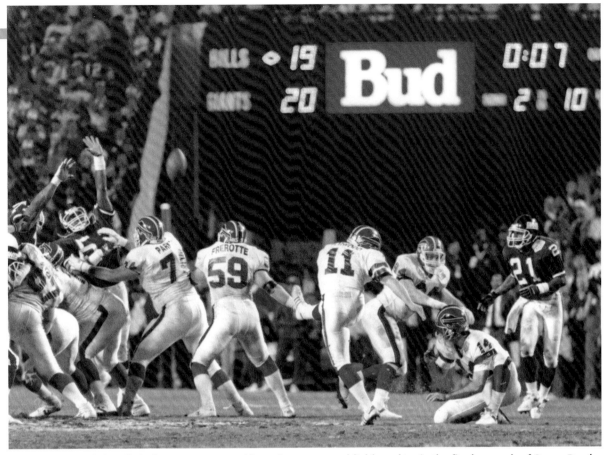

Near Miss *Buffalo Bills kicker Scott Norwood launches a 47-yard field-goal try in the final seconds of Super Bowl XXV. The kick was just a bit wide to the right, and the New York Giants hung on to win the game 20–19.*

points in its two National Football Conference (NFC) playoff wins, over the Chicago Bears (31–3) and the San Francisco 49ers (15–13); Buffalo had racked up 95 points in beating the Miami Dolphins (44–34) and the Los Angeles Raiders (51–3) for the American Football Conference (AFC) title.

The Giants' game plan hinged on keeping Bills quarterback Jim Kelly (b. 1960) and his no-huddle, quick-strike offense off the field for as long as possible. While its defense had to execute flawlessly, the key really was New York's ball-control offense. That meant efficient drives that took a lot of time—combining short passes from quarterback Jeff Hostetler (pressed into service six weeks earlier when starting quarterback Phil Simms injured his shoulder) and a huge effort from running back Otis Anderson.

The Giants maintained possession of the football for a Super Bowl-record 40 minutes, 33 seconds—more than two-thirds of the 60-minute game. Hostetler completed 20 of 32 passes, and Anderson rushed for 102 yards to earn the Most Valuable Player (MVP) award.

1991

Coach K Gets Big W

After falling short of a national championship in three consecutive trips to the NCAA Final Four, the Duke University Blue Devils men's basketball team beat the University of Kansas Jayhawks 72–65 at Indianapolis on April 1. It was the first national title for Duke and for its successful coach Mike Krzyzewski (b.1947), or Coach K, as he is known (because his name is difficult to say; it is actually pronounced sheh-SHEFFS-key).

When his team took the floor against the Kansas Jayhawks (22–7) in the final game, Coach K wondered if they would have enough energy after an emotional win two nights earlier against defending national-champion Nevada-Las Vegas (UNLV) in the semifinal game. The previous season, UNLV had dispatched the Blue Devils 103–73 in the most lopsided title game ever. In this year's tournament, though, Duke exacted revenge with a thrilling, 79–77 victory. UNLV had entered the game undefeated, ranked No. 1 in the country, and favored to win another title.

The Blue Devils quickly dispelled any doubts, shooting a torrid 59 percent in the first half to take a 42–34 lead at halftime. Hurley and Laettner again propelled the team, with a huge boost off the bench from guard Bill McCaffrey, who scored 16 points.

Kansas, meanwhile, shot inconsistently. Despite a valiant effort in the game's closing minutes, when Duke started to wear down, the Jayhawks couldn't get closer than five points. Duke was crowned national champions, and Coach K won the biggest game of all.

Bittersweet Cup Win

The Pittsburgh Penguins of the National Hockey League (NHL) ended 23 years of frustration by winning the team's first Stanley Cup on May 25 at the Met Center in Bloomington, Minnesota. The Penguins trounced the Minnesota North Stars, 8–0, to capture the Cup in game six of the best-of-seven finals. Pittsburgh superstar Mario Lemieux (b.1965), who had missed the first 50 games of the 80-game regular season due to a back injury, was the MVP of the playoffs.

Lemieux had five goals and seven assists in the finals, despite sitting out game three with back spasms. Since being drafted by the Penguins in 1984, Lemieux had earned the nickname Super Mario by winning two NHL scoring titles and the league's MVP honors in 1988.

As it goes in team sports, though, even the greatest players need support. The Penguins finally surrounded Lemieux with the right mix of talent for the 1990–1991 season, including rookie Jaromir Jagr, Mark Recchi, Paul Coffey, and goaltender Tom Barasso. Then they brought in coach Bob Johnson, who was executive director of USA Hockey and had led the University of Wisconsin to three NCAA hockey titles, to run the team.

Unfortunately, "Badger," as the coach was affectionately known, couldn't be around to help the Penguins defend their long-awaited Stanley Cup championship. In August, the Penguins' beloved coach was diagnosed with brain cancer. On November 26, six months before his team's triumph, he died.

The Bulls Run with Jordan

Michael Jordan (b.1963) had clearly achieved superstardom in the NBA well before the 1990–1991 season. He reigned supreme as the league's leading scorer all four previous seasons, and earned his first MVP award the year before. Yet as high as Jordan soared, there were always doubts and whispers. Could he lead the Chicago Bulls to an NBA championship?

Resounding cheers drowned out the whispers on June 12 when the Bulls claimed the team's very first NBA title by defeating the Los Angeles Lakers, 108–101, at the Great Western Forum in Los Angeles. Chicago lost the first game in the best-of-seven finals at home, then took four straight. Jordan, who averaged 31.2 points, 11.4 assists, and 6.6 rebounds per game for the series, was named the MVP—to go along with another regular-season scoring title and MVP trophy.

The finals included a marquee matchup between Jordan and the Lakers' Earvin "Magic" Johnson, owner of five championship rings. Neither superstar disappointed.

While Jordan performed his MVP feats, Johnson tried to carry the Lakers on his back. The 6-foot-9 point guard posted the 29th and 30th triple-doubles (double figures in scoring, rebounds, and assists) of his career, set a five-game finals record with 62 assists, and averaged 18.6 points and 8 rebounds per game.

Beyond their individual heroics, teamwork made the difference. Scottie Pippen (b.1965), Horace Grant, Bill Cartwright, B.J. Armstrong, and John Paxson provided the complements to Jordan's aerobatics that had been lacking when the Bulls lost the Eastern Conference Championship the previous two seasons. James Worthy, Byron Scott, A.C. Green, and other aging Lakers, meanwhile, couldn't muster the wizardry that had sparked the Lakers' five NBA titles during the 1980s.

The torch had officially been passed. "I'm not even thinking about any other championships right now," Jordan said during the Bulls' victory celebration. "I just want to enjoy this one for as long as I can."

Super Mario *Pittsburgh Penguins star Mario Lemieux holds the Stanley Cup aloft after leading his team to the first National Hockey League championship in franchise history.*

1991

It's a Bird, It's a Plane . . .

It's Mike Powell (b.1963), soaring to an incredible world record of 29 feet, 4 1/2 inches in the long jump on August 30. By two inches, he broke the 23-year-old mark set by Bob Beamon at the 1968 Summer Olympics in Mexico City—a record many considered unbeatable.

When Powell jogged into a hot and muggy National Stadium in Tokyo for the 1991 World Championships of Track and Field, few expected him to leap into the history books—except Powell, who, for metric-minded Japanese fans, had prophetically signed autographs with "8.95?"—that's meters, and 8.95 meters converts to 29 feet, 4 1/2 inches.

Yet before Powell entertained any thoughts of breaking Beamon's venerable record, he first had to contend with the here and now: the great Carl Lewis (b.1961). Lewis was not only the fastest man in the world (he set a world record in the 100-meter sprint at the same meet on August 25), but also the owner of back-to-back Olympic gold medals in the long jump at the 1984 and 1988 Games. Indeed, he was undefeated over a 10-year, 65-meet stretch. Powell, the Olympic silver medalist in 1988, hadn't beaten Lewis in 15 tries.

This all must have weighed heavily on Powell's mind, because the first four of his six jumps were relatively short compared to Lewis' efforts; three of Lewis' jumps were at least 29 feet (though he was aided by a wind at his back, so the jumps did not count for the record books). But on Powell's fifth jump, he summoned up every ounce of talent, frustration, and determination—and made the jump of his life.

Even as the crowd cheered the incredible eclipse of Beamon's record, Powell stood nervously awaiting Lewis' final jump. When it came up well short, the world officially had its new long jump superman.

Worst-to-First Double Play

The Minnesota Twins beat the visiting Atlanta Braves 1–0 in 10 innings in Game Seven on October 27 to cap one of the most exciting World Series ever.

Although the Twins were the champions, both teams were winners in a season in which they each executed remarkable turnarounds. Both teams had finished dead last in their respective divisions in 1990. And while hope springs eternal at the start of every baseball season, neither team could have anticipated their historic reversal of fortunes in 1991. There they stood, nonetheless, at the end of the 162-game regular season, alive and well in first place—the Twins atop the American League's West Division, the Braves kings of the National League's Western Division. Never before had any major league team gone from worst to first in consecutive seasons, and now two had done it in the same year.

The two teams then survived their league championship series and squared off in October in one of the most closely contested and entertaining World Series of all time. Four games were decided on the final pitch. Three went into extra innings. Five were decided by a single run.

Rickey Steals the Show

"Mayday" is the international call for help. Many baseball pitchers must have felt like shouting it whenever they saw Rickey Henderson lurking on first base. So it was only appropriate that on May 1—May Day around the world—Henderson became Major League Baseball's all-time stolen base leader, stealing base number 939 for his Oakland A's against the New York Yankees to break Lou Brock's record in a game at the Oakland-Alameda County Coliseum in California.

Born on Christmas Day in 1958 in Chicago, the gifted Henderson lent his unique package of baseball skills to eight different major league teams over a high-speed career that spanned 25 years through 2003. That included four stints with the Oakland Athletics, with whom he moved up from the minor leagues as a 21-year-old rookie in 1979.

Henderson quickly established himself as a complete, five-tool player: He hit for a high average and with home run power, fielded and threw the ball exceptionally well, and was a demon on the base paths. "He's the best lead-off hitter of all time, no question," former Yankees shortstop Tony Kubek told *The Sporting News* in 1986.

The key for the first batter in the lineup is to get on base, and Henderson mastered the art. A .279 lifetime hitter, he had 3,055 career hits. And he was just as happy to draw a walk. He did whatever it took to get on base, as his .401 career on-base percentage testifies.

But it was on base that he was most dangerous. The 10-time All-Star led the American League in stolen bases 12 times, most dramatically in 1982 when he set the single-season record with 130 steals. More than any other major leaguer, he eventually wound up crossing home plate: Henderson holds the record for runs scored, at 2,295. At age 44 in 2003, he played 30 games for the Los Angeles Dodgers. He finished the season at 1,406 career stolen bases. In 2009, he was inducted into the Baseball Hall of Fame.

Rickey Henderson

1991

The finale pitted Atlanta's 24-year-old John Smoltz against 36-year-old veteran Jack Morris, both pitching on just three days' rest. They each came out strong, throwing shutouts into the eighth inning. It looked like the Braves would score in the top half of the eighth inning, when Terry Pendleton smacked a ball into the gap in left-center field with Lonnie Smith on first base and no outs. But Smith hesitated coming around second base and had to hold up at third. The crafty Morris then pitched his way out of the inning.

The game remained scoreless after nine innings, and Morris kept on pitching—holding Atlanta scoreless in the top of the 10th inning. In the bottom of the inning, with one out and the bases loaded, Minnesota's Gene Larkin hit a fly ball that landed just beyond the infield, scoring Dan Gladden to win the game—and the World Series.

Morris, who won two of his three starts, was voted MVP of the series. In the end, the worst part was that one team had to lose.

Other Milestones of 1991

✔ American women skaters swept the World Figure Skating Championships in Munich, Germany, on March 16. Kristi Yamaguchi won the gold medal, Tonya Harding won the silver, and Nancy Kerrigan won the bronze.

✔ On March 30, the Northern Michigan University Wildcats captured their first NCAA Division I hockey title by beating the Boston University Terriers, 8–7, in triple overtime in the championship game.

✔ On July 28, the Montreal Expos' Dennis Martinez became the 14th big-league pitcher ever to toss a perfect game: 27 batters up and 27 batters down. Martinez shut down the Dodgers 2–0 in Los Angeles.

✔ On the same day that Rickey Henderson set his stolen base record (see page 23), May 1, 44-year-old

Desmond Howard

Nolan Ryan pitched his seventh career no-hitter, as the Texas Rangers blanked the Toronto Blue Jays, 3–0, at Arlington Stadium in Arlington, Texas.

✔ Unknown rookie John Daly won the Professional Golfers Association Championship on August 11 at Crooked Stick Golf Club in Carmel, Indiana. As the ninth alternate, the 25-year-old Daly was a long shot even to make it into the field, but he sailed to a three-stroke victory.

✔ On September 13, at the World Gymnastics Championships in Indianapolis, Kim Zmeskal, 15, became the first American to win the women's all-around title.

✔ On December 14, University of Michigan receiver Desmond Howard was awarded the Heisman Trophy as college football's best player for 1991.

Magic Retires

For many years, activists had raised awareness of the disease commonly known as AIDS (acquired immunodeficiency syndrome), although public perception remained that only certain segments of the population were at risk. That changed with a shocking announcement from Magic Johnson on November 7. The popular basketball star retired from the sport because he tested positive for HIV, the virus that causes AIDS.

The 31-year-old Johnson, who was still at the top of his game—he averaged 19.4 points, 7.0 rebounds, and 12.5 assists in his final full season in 1990–91—occasionally returned to the basketball court. Even in his retirement, fans voted him to the All-Star Game in the 1991–92 season, and he earned MVP honors in the West's 153–113 rout. He also played for the U.S. Olympic "Dream Team" in 1992, made an aborted comeback attempt in the 1992–93 preseason, coached the Los Angeles Lakers for part of the 1993–94 season, and played 32 games for the Lakers in 1995–96 before retiring for good.

You Goal, Girls!

Half a world away from home, in Tianhe Stadium in Guangzhou, China, the U.S. women's national soccer team scored two historic firsts on November 30. The team won the world's first women's World Cup Soccer Championship. They also became the first U.S. world champions in soccer since the game was introduced in America 128 years earlier.

On Top of the World *Michelle Akers and the United States' team won the first Women's World Cup in soccer.*

The title came after a heart-stopping 2–1 triumph over Norway. With three minutes remaining and the game tied, U.S. striker Michelle Akers kicked the decisive goal.

Akers (who scored the game's other goal too, giving her a team-high 10 goals in the six-game tournament) earned high praise from soccer legend Pelé, who led Brazil to three World Cup titles (1958, 1962, 1970). "I like her because she is intelligent, has presence of mind, and is often in the right position," he told reporters at the stadium. "She's fantastic."

1992

The Golden Girls

United States Olympians brought home a total of 11 medals from the Games of the XVI Winter Olympiad, held in Albertville, France, February 8 to 23. American women won nine of them, including all five of the United States' gold medals.

Leading the way was speed skater Bonnie Blair (b.1964) of Champaign, Illinois. The youngest in a family of five speed skating kids, she first laced up a pair of hand-me-down skates at the age of two and began competing when she was four.

At the 1988 Winter Olympics in Calgary, Alberta, she not only edged the defending East German champion in the 500-meter race—by two one-hundredths of a second—for the gold, but also set a world record. Blair won the event again in Albertville, by a more "comfortable" 18 one-hundredths of a second. Blair thus became the first U.S. woman to win a gold medal in two Olympics.

Four days later, with "Blair's Bunch" of 50 or so family and hometown friends, including her sponsors from the Champaign Police Department, cheering her on, she took the gold in the 1,000-meter race.

As did Blair growing up, many speed skaters start out racing in short-track competition, which was added to the Olympic slate of events in 1992. In short track, instead of racing in pairs against the clock, skaters race in a tight, bump-and-grind pack, usually four at a time—like roller derby on ice. The first to cross the finish line wins; elimination heats lead to semifinals and finals. In the finals, American Cathy Turner, who had taken an eight-year break from the sport from 1980 to 1988 to pursue a singing career, won the 500-meter race in a photo finish. With China's Li Yan ahead as they approached the finish line, Turner made a final kick and beat Li by four one-hundredths of a second, or about the length of a skate blade.

Kristi Yamaguchi (b.1971) laced up skates at Albertville, too, in the women's figure skating event. She arrived at the Games as one of two favorites, along with Japan's Midori Ito. The media hyped their contrasting styles: The more athletic Ito's repertoire featured explosive jumps; Yamaguchi was more polished and artistic. A former pairs skater who grew up clutching a Dorothy Hamill doll, Yamaguchi led after the first half of the

Good as Gold *American Kristi Yamaguchi overcame a fall in the freestyle program to win the women's figure skating competition at the Winter Olympic Games.*

competition, the short program, in which required moves are performed. Although she fell in the longer freestyle program, Ito did as well, and Yamaguchi skated away with the gold medal.

America's fifth golden girl, Donna Weinbrecht, won her medal on the snow, in a new Olympic sport: freestyle skiing. In the moguls event, competitors ski a run that is tightly packed with snow

1992

humps called moguls. Besides navigating the obstacle course cleanly, racers have to perform two airborne, or aerial, maneuvers. Weinbrecht grew up in New Jersey and taught herself the bumpy art of mogul skiing during the winter of 1985 in Vermont. At Albertville, racing in a snowstorm to the musical accompaniment of the Ramones' "Rock 'n' Roll High School," she narrowly beat Russian Yelizaveta Kozhevnikova for first place.

Duckpin History Rolls On

A Baltimore-born pastime slightly less well known than baseball (see the story on page 29) celebrated a new icon in 1992. On May 5, Pete Signore Jr. of North Haven, Connecticut, set a new world duckpin record by rolling a 279.

Duckpin is a century-old form of bowling that originated at Diamond Alleys in Baltimore—which happened to be owned by Wilbert Robinson and John J. McGraw, both of whom played for baseball's Baltimore Orioles in the early 1900s (they went on to become Hall of Fame managers with the Brooklyn Dodgers and New York Giants, respectively). Duckpins are sawed-off versions of traditional bowling pins. When the owners saw the way the small pins flew wildly around the alley, one of them remarked that it looked liked a "flock of flying ducks."

Duckpin bowlers use smaller balls (between five and six inches in diameter, versus the standard 8.59-inch bowling ball) and are allowed to roll three balls per turn. Played only in a handful of states, including Maryland, Connecticut, Indiana, and Massachusetts, duckpin and its enthusiasts have yet to bowl the elusive perfect 300 game.

Better Laettner than Never

In what many college basketball observers called the greatest game ever played, on March 28 the Duke University Blue Devils squeaked past the University of Kentucky Wildcats in the East Regional final of the men's NCAA tournament, 103–102. The one-point difference came in the closing 2.1 seconds of double overtime at the Spectrum in Philadelphia, when Duke's Christian Laettner snatched a long in-bounds pass from Grant Hill and nailed a miraculous 17-foot shot. The win sent the Blue Devils back to the Final Four in Minneapolis, where they went on to become the first repeat national champions in 19 years by handily defeating the University of Michigan in the final game, 71–51.

Laettner's magic moment at the Spectrum capped a classic game from the tournament's two best teams. They combined to make a phenomenal 61 percent of their shots. Still, all the precision passing, deft dribbling, and sharp shooting boiled down to the last two nail-biting possessions. After the Wildcats' Sean Woods banked in an off-balance running shot for the lead with 2.5 seconds remaining, it looked as if coach Rick Pitino's Kentucky team would be heading for the finals. But Laettner had other ideas.

The Blue Devils' center had already registered a perfect offensive performance. He was nine for nine from the field and 10 for 10 from the free-throw line. He caught Hill's pass with his back to basket, dribbled once, spun around, stopped, and popped—swish!

Old Is New Again

On April 6, the Baltimore Orioles took baseball back to the future. Hosting the season's home opener, the team christened its new ballpark, Oriole Park at Camden Yards. Besides generating rave reviews and sold-out crowds, the stadium became the prototype for a new generation of "retro" venues around Major League Baseball. (For the record, the Orioles beat the Cleveland Indians 2–0 in that first game behind right-hander Rick Sutcliffe's five-hitter.)

Camden Yards, constructed on 85-acres at a cost of $110 million, has state-of-the-art scoreboards, grandstands, concessions, clubhouses, and other amenities. Yet it is designed in the style of charming, turn-of-the-20th-century, downtown ballparks that were integral centers of their communities. Steel, rather than concrete trusses, an arched brick facade, a sun roof over the sloped upper deck, an asymmetrical playing field, and a natural grass field are some of the nostalgic niceties.

Ebbets Field (Brooklyn Dodgers), Fenway Park (Boston Red Sox), Crosley Field (Cincinnati Reds), Wrigley Field (Chicago Cubs), and the Polo Grounds (New York Giants) were among the ballparks that served as powerful influences in the design of Oriole Park. Other retro parks that followed Camden Yards' lead over the next decade were Jacobs Field (Cleveland Indians), Comerica Park (Detroit Tigers), Safeco Field (Seattle Mariners), Minute Maid Field (Houston Astros), SBC Park (San Francisco Giants), and Great American Ballpark (Reds).

Magic Moment   *Co-captain Earvin "Magic" Johnson celebrates the U.S. men's basketball team's gold medal at the Olympics. NBA players were allowed to compete in the Games for the first time.*

Women in Hoops Hall

Two women who were ahead of their time on the hardwood—Nera White and Lucia Harris-Stewart—were inducted into the Naismith Memorial Basketball Hall of Fame on May 11.

White brought athleticism not often seen in the women's game in the 1950s and 1960s to her Nashville Business College (NBC) team and the United States

1992

National Team. She led NBC to 10 Amateur Athletic Union (AAU) national championships between 1955 and 1969, and was named the Outstanding Player of the tournament 10 times. In 1957–58, she helped the American team win the World Basketball Championship in Rio de Janeiro, Brazil, where she earned tournament MVP honors.

Harris-Stewart was the dominant center of her time (the mid-1970s). In her college career at Delta State, she averaged 25.9 points and 14.4 rebounds per game while helping the school win 109 of 115 games. Delta State won three consecutive Association for Intercollegiate Athletics for Women (AIAW) basketball titles beginning in 1975. Harris-Stewart also was

World's Greatest Female Athlete *American Jackie Joyner-Kersee left no doubt about it when she won the heptathlon at the Summer Olympic Games for the second consecutive time. (see page 32)*

the leading scorer and rebounder for the United States team that earned a silver medal at the 1976 Olympics.

The Dream Team

Barcelona, Spain, hosted the 1992 Summer Games, July 24 to August 9, with 9,370 of the world's best athletes competing in 257 events. A total of 169 nations competed. They included South Africa, which had been banned since 1960 for its apartheid policy, but had finally abandoned its racist social structure. A single German team appeared for the first time since Word War II, following the tearing down of the Berlin Wall. And there was a Unified Team comprising several former republics of the Soviet Union, which had collapsed in 1991.

This was the last year both the Winter and Summer Olympic Games were held in the same year, as they had been since the modern Olympics began in 1896. After 1992, the games were switched to a staggered schedule. The next Winter Games were held just two years later, in Lillehammer, Norway, and thereafter every four years. The next Summer Games were held four years later in Atlanta, Georgia.

For the first time, the International Olympic Committee opened men's basketball to professional players instead of only amateurs. USA Basketball, the governing body for hoops in the United States, responded by forming the Dream Team. Coached by the Detroit Pistons' Chuck Daly and co-captained by Magic Johnson and Larry Bird (b.1956), the team also starred Charles Barkley (b.1963),

Dan and Dave and Dollars

Commercialism at the 1992 Olympics wasn't confined to basketball players. A couple of decathletes made financial headlines, too. Reebok International, a maker of sneakers and other sports apparel, signed Dan O'Brien (b.1966) and Dave Johnson to star in a $25 million advertising campaign, which humorously followed their rivalry to qualify for the U.S. Olympic Team. Dan was the reigning world champion in the 10-part, two-day decathlon; Dave held the record for the highest second-day score. One seemed destined to emerge as the world's greatest athlete.

At the qualifying meet for Olympics, however, Dan failed in the pole vault event and didn't make the team—thus suddenly canceling the Dan and Dave rivalry. Dave settled for the bronze medal in Barcelona, while Reebok was forced to revamp its ads. Undaunted, Dan set a new world record a month later at a meet in France.

Clyde Drexler, Patrick Ewing (b.1962), Michael Jordan, Karl Malone (b.1963), Chris Mullin, Scottie Pippen, David Robinson (b.1965), John Stockton (b.1962), and Duke University's Christian Laettner (see page 28).

The presence of Johnson, who had retired from the NBA the previous year after announcing that he was HIV-positive (see page 25), was a boost for people everywhere suffering from the dread disease. The fact that Johnson was still healthy and on his game, and that he still had legions of fans worldwide, did much to lift the sprits of those who had felt shunned and hopeless.

Arguably the greatest basketball team ever assembled, the Dream Team was criticized as being a grandiose display of pampered millionaires—a team that exemplified the big-business and mega-marketing elements that enveloped sports during the 1990s. (Coincidentally, NBA Commissioner David Stern was named 1992's most powerful man in sports in *The Sporting News'* annual top 100 listing.) The fact that the team elected to stay in a $900-a-night luxury hotel rather than the more modest Olympic Village with the rest of the world's athletes only fueled the fire. Four members of the team failed to show up for the Opening Ceremony. "It's very much like traveling with 12 rock stars," Daly remarked.

Wrote Tom Callahan of *U.S. News & World Report* in his post-Games analysis, "At the Olympic Games, where the truest dreamers have been swallowed up by a sensation, the Dream Team represents reality as much as anything else, although it also represents Reebok, Nike, and the United States. Commercialism and professionalism have attended the games for decades—for centuries, truth to tell—but never before have they carried the flag or the day, and the reality is a sensation."

To no one's surprise, the Dream Team dazzled. They went undefeated in eight basketball games, scored more than 100 points in every one, and averaged a record-setting 117.25 points per game. They never called a timeout. The average margin of victory was 43.75 points, and the closest contest was over Croatia, 117–85, for the gold medal.

1992

Jackie of All Trades

It's easy to see why Jackie Joyner-Kersee is considered by many to be the greatest female athlete ever. Just check out her trophy case. Hanging front and center are six Olympic medals, two of them golds won back to back at the 1988 and 1992 Summer Games in the grueling seven-event, two-day heptathlon, and another gold for the long jump in 1988. There are trophies, medals, and newspaper clippings from her days as an All-America basketball star at the University of California at Los Angeles (UCLA), and when she was a three-sport standout at her hometown high school in East St. Louis, Illinois. What makes Joyner-Kersee's accomplishments even more impressive is that the multi-sport star has asthma.

Born on March 3, 1962, she was named after then President John F. Kennedy's wife, Jacqueline. "If you had asthma, they said you couldn't run or do some of the other things I was doing," said Joyner-Kersee, recalling when she was diagnosed with the disease at age 18. Undeterred, she went on to become the first lady of track and field in the United

Other Milestones of 1992

✔ On April 8, tennis star Arthur Ashe (1943–1993) revealed that since 1988 he had been HIV-positive and that he now had AIDS.

✔ The University of Arkansas won its ninth consecutive NCAA men's indoor track and field championship on May 14.

✔ In the NBA, the Chicago Bulls successfully defended their league championship from 1991 by beating the Portland Trailblazers in six games in the Finals. The two teams split the opening two games in Chicago, then the Bulls won two of three games in Portland. In the decisive Game Six in Chicago on June 14, the Bulls rallied for a 97–93 win. The Bulls' Michael Jordan was the Finals MVP.

Dave Winfield

✔ The NBA's Larry Bird retired on August 18. In 13 seasons, all with the Boston Celtics, he made 10 All-Star teams and won three MVP awards.

✔ On September 20, Philadelphia Phillies second baseman Mickey Morandini turned the first unassisted triple play in baseball's National League since May 30, 1927, in a 13-inning, 3–2 loss to the Pirates in Pittsburgh.

✔ The Toronto Blue Jays beat the Atlanta Braves in six games in the World Series. In the final game, on October 24 in Atlanta, Dave Winfield's two-out, two-run double in the 11th inning broke a 2–2 tie and propelled the Blue Jays to a 4–3 victory.

States, making her first Olympic team in 1984 and earning a silver medal in the heptathlon at the Los Angeles Games that year.

Joyner-Kersee (she married her UCLA track coach, Bob Kersee, in 1986) dominated the event for the next four years, winning all nine heptathlons she entered. The first woman to break the 7,000-point mark, she set world records twice again before eclipsing them all, scoring 7,291 points at the 1988 Games in Seoul, South Korea. She finished her Olympic career at the 1996 Games in Atlanta, where she took the bronze in the long jump.

King Richard Abdicates

Long Live the King *As colorful as he was successful, Richard Petty retired from active NASCAR competition with a host of awards and a legion of fans.*

After a record 200 career race victories, including seven Daytona 500 wins, and seven season points championships (tied for another record), Richard Petty (b.1937) drove in his final NASCAR race at the Hooters 500 on November 15 at Atlanta Motor Speedway.

"The King," as stock car racing's most popular and successful driver had become known, was hanging up his crown (actually, a black cowboy hat, along with dark sunglasses) after a remarkable driving career that spanned 35 years. He finished 35th in his familiar No. 43 car at the Hooters 500 after getting tangled up in a fiery crash with Dick Trickle, Ken Schrader, and Darrell Waltrip. Still, the fans witnessed a great race. At the start, six drivers had a chance to earn enough points to win the season's Winston Cup Championship. It came down to Bill Elliott and Alan Kulwicki. Elliott won the race, but Kulwicki's second-place was enough to capture the year's title (the season championship, determined by finishes in a year's worth of races).

The same day the King bade farewell, a young prince emerged. Finishing 31st in his first Winston Cup event was rookie Jeff Gordon (b.1971). Before the decade was out, Gordon captured three Cup titles and led the series in wins five consecutive years (1995–1999). NASCAR racing had found a new member of its "royal" family.

1993

The Reich Stuff

The Buffalo Bills engineered the largest comeback in NFL history when they overcame a 32-point, third-quarter deficit to beat the Houston Oilers 41–38 in overtime in an AFC Wild-Card Playoff Game (1992 season) at Rich Stadium in Buffalo on January 3.

What's more, the Bills, winners of the last two AFC championships, did it without starting quarterback Jim Kelly, who was injured. Backup quarterback Frank Reich engineered the comeback, though Reich was no stranger to big rallies: He's the guy who led the University of Maryland back from a 31–0 halftime deficit against the University of Miami in 1984 to a 42–40 victory—the greatest comeback in college football history.

Houston, which finished 10–6 during the regular season, and Buffalo, which was 11–5, had just squared off just a week earlier in the last game of the regular season, and the Oilers humiliated the Bills, 27–3. So by halftime in the playoff game, when the Oilers went comfortably into the locker room with a 28–3 lead, it looked like a repeat blowout. Instead, Houston simply blew it.

First, though, the Oilers actually increased their lead with an interception return for a touchdown in the opening moments of the third quarter. With the score 35–3, thousands of the hometown fans began streaming to the exits. They soon wish they had stayed.

Buffalo began its comeback with a 1-yard touchdown run by Kenneth Davis. After the Bills recovered an onside kick, Reich teamed with Don Beebe on a 38-yard touchdown pass. Suddenly, the score was 35–17 with half of the third quarter still remaining.

That was enough time for Reich and Andre Reed to hook up on a pair of touchdown passes to make it 35–31 going into the final period. And when Reed caught another touchdown pass from Reich in the fourth quarter to put the Bills ahead 38–35, their fans were as delirious as the Oilers were dazed. Houston tied the game in the closing moments of regulation time, but in overtime the Bills intercepted a Warren Moon (b.1956) pass, which set up Steve Christie's 32-yard, game-winning field goal.

It was all for naught, though, as the Bills lost their third straight Super Bowl later in January.

Bull Run *Superstar Michael Jordan and the Bulls made it three NBA championships in a row (see page 37).*

Timing Is Everything

On April 5 in the New Orleans Superdome, with 20 seconds remaining in the NCAA men's basketball tournament final and the University of North Carolina clinging to a 73–71 lead, All-America forward Chris Webber of the University of Michigan rebounded a missed free throw, dribbled down the court, and called for a time-out. Except the Michigan Wolverines were out of time-outs—and now out of luck. Michigan was assessed a two-shot technical foul and Carolina went on to win, 77–71.

Webber's mistake not only effectively ended the game, but also the run of Michigan's fabled Fab Five. A year earlier, Webber headlined a quintet of highly touted freshman. He and Juwan Howard, Jalen Rose, Ray Jackson, and Jimmy King lived up to the hype and reached the 1992 finals, only to lose to a more experienced Duke University team. The preseason favorites in the 1992–93 college season, Michigan finished its regular schedule

35

King of the Court

Tennis star Arthur Ashe was just 49 when he died of AIDS on February 6, leaving behind a legacy of on-court achievement, civic contribution, and social justice.

Ashe was the first African American to win the men's singles title at the U.S. Open (in 1968) and at Wimbledon (1975), and he was the first to play in the Davis Cup (in 1963). In all, he won 33 career singles championships, including three Grand Slams, and 18 doubles titles. He compiled a stellar career singles record of 816–260 before suffering a heart attack in 1979 that eventually led to his retirement.

Ashe was much more than a great tennis player, however. Even before being diagnosed with AIDS—he contracted the virus that causes the disease from a blood transfusion—he fought for social causes such as ending South African apartheid (the official practice of racial segregation and discrimination). In his post-playing career, he championed issues such as heathcare, education, and AIDS awareness.

ranked third in the nation, with a 26–4 record and a number-one seed in the NCAA tournament.

It took a pair of overtime wins, against UCLA and the University of Kentucky, but the Fab Five advanced to the finals with UNC coach Dean Smith's (b.1931) 28–4 Tar Heels. It was Webber's final collegiate game. A month later he announced that he would enter the NBA draft. This time, his timing was right: He was the number-one pick.

Lady Jordan

"If Michael Jordan has a clone, it's Sheryl Swoopes." Those lofty words of praise were spoken on April 2 by Vanderbilt University women's basketball coach Jim Foster—and for good reason.

Swoopes had just blistered his top-ranked Commodores for 31 points in leading the Texas Tech Lady Red Raiders to a 60–46 victory in the semifinals of the 1993 NCAA women's Final Four.

In true Jordan-esque fashion, two nights later in the championship game against Ohio State, Swoopes scored more points than the entire Vanderbilt team, racking up 47 points in an 84–82 thriller. Swoopes tallied the most points that any player, male or female, ever managed in an NCAA final.

"When it was over, my first thought was, 'Is this real?'" she said in a post-game interview with the *Washington Post.* "At times, I get it in my mind that there is no way I can miss." Swoopes, a senior, became the second woman ever drafted by the all-male U.S. Basketball League.

Selected by the Daytona Beach Hooters, she opted to go to Europe, where she played 10 games in an Italian league. In 1997, Swoopes joined the Women's National Basketball Association's Houston Comets, where she continued her winning ways.

Jordan's Surprise

In retrospect, the 1992–93 NBA season might have seemed routine to the guy who had to scale the rafters of Chicago Stadium to hang another banner. Or to whomever made the trophy for the league's leading scorer. Yet the road to the Chicago Bulls' third consecutive championship and Michael Jordan's seventh straight scoring title was anything but routine.

Collectively, the Bulls didn't have much trouble capturing the Central Division title again, with a 57–25 record, although they lost the coveted home-court advantage throughout the playoffs to the New York Knicks, who finished 60–22. Jordan, meanwhile, had to deal with the intense media scrutiny that grew from published reports of his gambling excesses and late-night forays.

The Bulls swept the Atlanta Hawks and the Cleveland Cavaliers in the first two rounds of the playoffs in May, then had their hands full with coach Pat Riley's (b.1945) tough Knicks squad.

Led by center Patrick Ewing (b.1962) and the league's best defense, New York won the first two games of the series at home. The Bulls answered right back and took two in Chicago, with Jordan scoring 54 points in game four.

In the pivotal game five back in New York's Madison Square Garden, Chicago won 97–94. An infamous closing-moments sequence—in which Knicks forward Charles Smith missed several

One-Woman Show *Sheryl Swoopes (center) was an unstoppable force in the NCAA title game, scoring 47 points in Texas Tech's win.*

1993

point-blank chances to win the game—saved the Bulls' season.

The 4–2 series victory catapulted Chicago back into the NBA Finals, where the Bulls met the Phoenix Suns in June. Behind newly acquired Charles Barkley and sharp-shooters Danny Ainge and Dan Majerle, the Suns had gone 62–20 during the regular season, giving them homecourt advantage. But Jordan and the Bulls reversed that fortune by winning the first two games in Phoenix.

Game three was one of the most memorable postseason games in NBA history, with the Suns prevailing 129–121 in an epic, triple-overtime marathon. But Phoenix couldn't withstand Jordan's 55-point outburst in game four and eventually succumbed in six games. "Winning this championship was harder than anything I've done before in basketball," Jordan said.

His off-the-court life was about to become incredibly harder. On July 23, his beloved father—whom he often called his best friend—was murdered in North Carolina. Three months later, on October 6, still grief-stricken and increasingly disenchanted with the life of a public megastar, Jordan shocked the sports world by announcing his retirement. At age 30 and with nine years of history-making basketball behind him, he called it quits—for the first time, but certainly not the last—while still at the top of his over-the-top game.

"I feel that at this particular time in my career I have reached the pinnacle of my career," Jordan said in his 1993 retirement press conference. "I have achieved a lot in that short amount of time, but I just feel I don't have anything else for myself to prove."

Ecstasy and Agony

Colonial Affair won the 125th running of the Belmont Stakes in Belmont, New York, on June 5. But the real story wasn't so much the horse as it was the jockey. Colonial Affair was ridden to victory by Julie Krone (b.1963). Krone became the first woman to ride a winner in a Triple Crown race.

The victory was the crowning achievement of Krone's stellar racing career. The winningest female jockey in horse racing history, she had raced hundreds of times at the famous track, including three other Belmont Stakes, so she was familiar with the venue. This time, it counted the most. "I turned for home and told myself, 'Now I'm going to win the Belmont Stakes,'" she said afterward.

In 2000, she became the first woman to be inducted into the National Thoroughbred Racing Hall of Fame. "I wish I could put every one of you here on a race horse at the eighth pole, so you could have the same feeling that I did," Krone said at the ceremony in Saratoga Springs, New York. "I got to do something I love so much every day. And today I know for sure that life doesn't get any better."

The Rarest of No-Hitters

Since St. Louis Brown Stockings righthander George "Grin" Bradley became the first Major League Baseball pitcher to do it, on July 15, 1876, pitching a no-hit baseball game has remained a remarkable personal achievement. But as hard as it is to pitch a complete game with no hits, they're not all that uncommon. At least one no-hitter has been thrown in all

Tall in the Saddle

When he retired from baseball at the end of the 1993 season, Lynn Nolan Ryan, Jr. was 46 years old and still pitching 95 miles per hour. After pitching in the major leagues for 27 years, the gentleman rancher born on January 31, 1947, in Refugio, Texas, rode into the sunset holding more than 50 records, including most no-hitters (seven), most career strikeouts (5,714), and most strikeouts in a season (383 in 1973). Throwing heat over four decades for four teams (the New York Mets, California Angels, Houston Astros, and Texas Rangers), Ryan retired with 324 wins against 292 losses. He started more games (773) than anyone except Cy Young (815). He never won a Cy Young Award, but was inducted into the Baseball Hall of Fame in 1999.

In the May 1993 issue of *Texas Monthly* magazine, Joe Nick Petoski wrote a piece entitled "A Farewell to Arm," a sort of open letter to Ryan. Petoski's prose summed up Ryan, not so much in baseball terms, but in what he meant to the game, those who love it, and the state of Texas.

"I thought I would drop you this thank-you note—not so much for all the records you've shattered and all the milestones you've reached; not for all you've done for baseball in Texas, bringing excitement to the Astros a few years back and respectability to the Rangers today; not for being a walking, talking advertisement for the benefits of rigorous training and clean living; and certainly not for being a celebrity so inextricably tied to our state

that two roads—one in Arlington, between Houston and Freeport, near your hometown of Alvin—have been named the Nolan Ryan Expressway. The real reason I wanted to thank you was for being my seven-year-old's first hero. I couldn't have asked for a better role model. It's not just that you are a 46-year-old adult who plays a kid's game for a living, excelling in all aspects of your position—though that would be more than enough. You married your high school sweetheart. You raised your family in

Nolan Ryan

the same town in which you grew up. You're a cattleman—what could be more Texan? And rarely is heard a disparaging word about you. Years from now you may be exposed as a crank and a whiner, a showboat with a big head, or just another money-grubbing jock. But I'm not betting on it. From where I sit in the grandstand, you appear to be a class act, the last in a long line of good guys who seem to have vanished from your profession."

1993

but three major league seasons (1982, 1989, 2000) since 1960. But the 2–0 no-hitter pitched on September 4, 1993, at Yankee Stadium by New York Yankees lefthander Jim Abbott is the only one of its kind.

It's not because Abbott shut down an explosive Cleveland Indians' lineup, featuring such All-Star hitters as Kenny Lofton, Albert Belle, Manny Ramirez, and Jim Thome—who just six days earlier had pounded him for 10 hits and seven runs in an inning and a third. Or because he struck out only three hitters but walked five, and each time wriggled out of trouble. It's because he has only one hand.

His entire life, Abbott had said "no" to accepting pity or being treated differently because he was born without a right hand. And he wouldn't take no for an answer when challenged to prove he belonged on the pitcher's mound. At age 11, in his Little League pitching debut, he threw a no-hitter. He pitched the gold-medal-winning game against Japan in the 1988 Olympics. And without a day in the minor leagues, he jumped directly from the University of Michigan to the California Angels' starting rotation.

"I don't think I'm handicapped," Abbott told *Sports Illustrated for Kids* in 1994. "My hand hasn't kept me from doing anything I wanted to do. I believe you can do anything you want, if you put your mind to it."

Ryding High in England

Golf challenges an individual's physical and mental skills. It's each golfer for himself or herself up and down the fairways and putting greens. But every two years, the top American professional male golfers team up to compete against Europe's best pros in the Ryder Cup. There are no money prizes for the winners, only national pride and transatlantic bragging rights. So when the U.S. team rallied on the last day of the 1993 Ryder Cup—contested at The Belfry in Sutton Coldfield, England, September 24 to 26—the Stars and Stripes unfurled proudly.

Golf is considered a gentlemanly sport, with strictly enforced rules of play and etiquette. There's no trash talking between opponents. Things got a bit testy two years earlier, however, when the matches were held at Kiawah Island in South Carolina (the site alternates between the United States and Europe). Tensions ran high, with the post-Desert Storm Americans feeling patriotic (they donned camouflage caps one day), European charges of cheating, and other back-and-forth head games.

Now, the competition at The Belfry boiled down to the last day. The Americans trailed late in the competition, but Ryder Cup rookie Davis Love III pulled out a critical victory over Constantino Rocca, and the U.S. team won 15-13. America got the Cup back for the first time since 1983. Graciously, both teams accepted the outcome.

Carter's Clout

Almost every kid that grows up watching baseball dreams of one day hitting the home run that wins the World Series for his team. In big-league history, though, only two players ever

Other Milestones of 1993

✔ On February 3, cantankerous Cincinnati Reds owner Marge Schott was suspended from baseball for one year and fined $25,000 for making derogatory racial and ethnic remarks.

✔ President Bill Clinton issued Proclamation 6527, declaring February 4 National Women and Girls in Sports Day. The proclamation recognized the achievements of women in the field of sports and their efforts to break down sexual and racial barriers.

Don Shula

✔ Major League Baseball welcomed two new teams, the Florida Marlins and the Colorado Rockies, on April 5.

✔ On September 7, St. Louis Cardinals outfielder Mark Whiten became the 12th Major League Baseball player to hit four home runs in a single game.

✔ Miami Dolphins head coach Don Shula won his NFL-record 325th game with a 19–14 victory over the Philadelphia Eagles in Philadelphia on November 14.

have hit a walk-off home run to end the World Series. The first was Pittsburgh's Bill Mazeroski, against the Yankees in the Fall Classic in 1960. The next came this year, on October 23, when the Toronto Blue Jays' Joe Carter (b.1960) connected off Philadelphia Phillies reliever Mitch Williams for a three-run home run in the bottom of the ninth inning to win game six 8–6 and give his team a four games to two win in the Series.

The left-handed Williams, the Phillies' hard-throwing closing pitcher, had recorded a career-high 43 saves during the regular season.

But "the Wild Thing" had been living up to his wicked-fastball-shaky-control nickname in the series, saving game two, then blowing game four. On this day, with Philadelphia winning 6–5, Williams walked Rickey Henderson to lead off the ninth inning, induced a fly out, then gave up a single to Paul Molitor (b.1956). Carter worked the count to 2–2 as the raucous Skydome crowd urged him on. Williams wound up, delivered…and so did Carter, sending the ball over the left-field fence. The Blue Jays won!

Toronto, which beat Atlanta in the 1992 World Series (see page 32), thus became the first team to win back-to-back World Series since the New York Yankees in 1977–78.

1994

Seminoles Win Two Close Ones

The New Year started out doubly nice for Florida State University's football team. First, the Seminoles pulled out a dramatic, 18–16 victory over the University of Nebraska in the Orange Bowl in Miami on January 1. Then, a day later, the team was voted national champions for the first time in school history.

Florida State won its game when freshman Scott Bentley kicked a 22-yard field goal with 24 seconds left, and Nebraska's Byron Bennett misfired on a 45-yard try as time ran out. The Fighting Irish of the University of Notre Dame also won on New Year's Day, edging Texas A&M University, 24–21, in the Cotton Bowl. What's more, back on November 13, Notre Dame had beaten Florida State. The Irish finished the season with a 11–1 record, Florida State with a 12–1 record. On the strength of their head-to-head win, Notre Dame head coach Lou Holtz (b.1937) complained that the Irish should have been ranked number one.

So it goes in the always-spinning world of sports debates. This one will probably rage forever.

Super Bowl XXVII: 2–0 vs. 0–4

There are winners and there are losers. And somewhere in between are the Buffalo Bills. Remarkably, they reached the Super Bowl for an unprecedented fourth year in a row. More incredibly, with a 30–13 rout at the hands of the Dallas Cowboys on January 30 at the Georgia Dome in Atlanta, the Bills lost their fourth Super Bowl in a row—also unprecedented.

While Buffalo was left to ponder their triumphs and tragedies, Dallas hoisted the Lombardi Trophy for the second straight year. The Cowboys had whipped these same Bills in Super Bowl XXVI, 52–17. Dallas now joined the Green Bay Packers, Miami Dolphins, Pittsburgh Steelers (who did it twice), and San Francisco 49ers as the only teams to win back-to-back Super Bowls.

The rematch favored the Cowboys. Despite losing their first two regular-season games and overcoming injuries to quarterback Troy Aikman (b.1966) and running back Emmitt Smith (b.1969), the Cowboys went 12–4 to win the NFC East. They sailed through the playoffs, dispens-

Gooooooaaaaaaaaaal! *The United States stunned heavily favored Colombia in soccer's World Cup (see page 47).*

ing the Packers and the 49ers. Buffalo finished 12–4 as well to capture the AFC East, then beat the Los Angeles Raiders and the Kansas City Chiefs in the playoffs. Still, they were considered the underdogs against the reigning NFL champs.

The Bills led at halftime, 13–6, but fell apart from there under the Cowboys' speedy, powerful defense and their massive offensive line. Buffalo turned the ball over three times, including a costly third-quarter fumble by runningback Thurman Thomas that was returned 46 yards for a touchdown. Smith, on the merit of his 132 rushing yards and two touchdowns, was named the game's MVP.

Winter Wonderland

The XXVII Olympic Winter Games were held in idyllic Lillehammer, Norway, February 12 to 27. The friendly, well-organized venue and outstanding athletic achievements combined for one

1994

of the most successful Olympics ever. The United States brought home 13 medals—six gold, five silver, and two bronze—while host Norway doubled that total to win the most medals at the Games.

Although the women's figure skating competition generated the juiciest headlines (see page 45), the speed skating events best epitomized the genuine Olympic spirit. Norway's own Johann Koss wowed the home crowd by winning three golds—in the 1,500-meter, 5,000-meter, and 10,000-meter races. American skater Bonnie Blair took her third straight Olympic title in the 500-meter sprint and second straight in the 1,000-meter race. Her trove of five gold medals, dating back to the 1988 Calgary Games, are the most won by an American female athlete in either summer or winter.

Unlike Blair, Dan Jansen (b.1965) appeared to be cursed in Olympic competition. One of the greatest sprinters in speed skating history, he had won the world sprint championship twice, won seven overall World Cup titles, and set seven world records. Yet he failed to win any medal at the 1984 Olympics. Four years later, at the Winter Games in Calgary, Jansen was distraught over the death of his sister the day of the 500-meter final, and he slipped and fell during the race. The same thing happened in the 1,000-meter race.

Jansen finished out of the medals again at the 1992 Albertville Games. Unbelievably, he slipped in the 500-meter in Lillehammer and finished eighth. His last chance came in the 1,000-meter race. Powered by what he would later describe in his autobiography, *Full Circle*, as "a jolt

of energy" in his legs, Jansen not only finished in first place, but set a world record. With fans of every nation cheering, he skated a victory lap around the Viking Ship oval with his infant daughter, named after his late sister, Jane, in his arms—and a hard-earned gold medal around his neck.

A comparatively unknown American came out of nowhere to win the gold medal in the men's downhill skiing event. Tommy Moe, a skiing prodigy from Montana, had never even won a World Cup race before hitting the slopes in Lillehammer. Thirty thousand Norwegians watched in agony as Moe edged native son Kjetil Andre Aamodt by four one-hundredths of a second for the gold medal. The blow was later softened when it was learned that Moe's great-great grandfather was Norwegian.

Gretzky's Number One

On March 23, before a packed house at The Forum in Inglewood, California, the Los Angeles Kings' Wayne Gretzky officially became the greatest goal scorer in the history of the National Hockey League.

It had been obvious for some time that Gretzky eventually would pass the great Gordie Howe—his boyhood idol—atop the league's all-time goal-scoring chart. Gretzky already had passed "Mr. Hockey" as the top points scorer (goals plus assists) several seasons earlier. His pursuit of the goals record became hockey's version of Hank Aaron chasing Babe Ruth for baseball's all-time career home-run record.

On March 20, Gretzky tied Howe with career goal No. 801, in a game against the San Jose Sharks. The next time the Kings took the ice was three nights later, against the Vancouver Canucks.

In the second period, Gretzky took a pass from long-time teammate Marty McSorley and shot the puck past Canucks' goaltender Kirk McLean for the historic goal.

Gretzky, whose career began in the World Hockey Association in 1978, would go on to play through the 1998–99 season and finish with 894 career goals.

Rangers End a 53-Year Freeze-Out

The New York Rangers won the Stanley Cup in 1940. Not until June 14 of this year did they again possess the National Hockey League's championship trophy. No NHL team or fans had ever waited so long, and the Rangers ended their drought in thrilling fashion.

Haunted by its cursed past, the team began a serious rebuilding effort in 1991 by acquiring Mark Messier (b.1961), who had been captain of the Edmonton Oilers

As the Skates Turn

You can't make this stuff up, unless perhaps for a sleazy soap-opera script. That's pretty much what the sordid Olympic tale of archrival figure skaters Tonya Harding and Nancy Kerrigan seemed like.

Scene 1: Our story opens just after Christmas 1993. Harding, her ex-husband, and two other shady characters conspire to attack and injure Kerrigan—the reigning U.S. champion, Olympic favorite, and thorn in Harding's side—to keep her from competing in the upcoming U.S. Skating Championships.

Scene 2: On January 6, following a practice session in Detroit, Kerrigan is clubbed on her right knee. The unknown attacker flees. Two days later, Harding wins the national title, from which the injured Kerrigan has had to withdraw. Kerrigan is named to the team anyway.

Scene 3: Several witnesses come forward and tip off FBI agents about the plot. Arrests follow, though Harding is spared. She denies any knowledge or involvement, until her ex-hubby cuts a deal with the Feds and squeals on her. Harding finally confesses that she knew he was involved, but found out only after the attack. She sues the U.S. Olympic Committee (USOC) to prevent it from kicking her off the Olympic team. The USOC blinks, and the Tonya and Nancy Show shifts to Norway.

Scene 4: Kerrigan leads after the short program, Harding is in 10th place, and CBS basks in the sixth highest-rated television broadcast of all time. On February 25, petite Ukranian teenager Oksana Baiul edges Kerrigan for the gold. On the medal stand, silver-medalist Kerrigan, unaware her microphone is on, makes snotty remarks about Baiul. Harding, who finished eighth, is nowhere to be found.

Epilogue: Kerrigan turns pro, gets involved with a married man, and skates in ice shows. Harding pleads guilty to conspiracy, is banned from competition, and, years later, becomes a celebrity boxer.

O.J. Runs
Out of Bounds

Orenthal James "O.J." Simpson (b.1947) was a marvel to watch on the football field. As an All-America running back for the University of Southern California, he won the 1968 Heisman Trophy. Over 11 seasons in the NFL (1969–1979), the first nine with the Buffalo Bills, he amassed 11,236 rushing yards—including a then-record 2,003 yards in 1973. He won the league's MVP award that year. When he retired from football, Simpson segued from football player to affable broadcaster, actor, and television pitchman.

On June 17, the nation marveled at TV images of O.J. on the run again, only this time in a white Ford Bronco being chased by the Los Angeles Police Department (LAPD). Simpson finally surrendered and was charged with the stabbing murders of his ex-wife Nicole Brown Simpson and her friend Ronald Goldman, whose bodies were found on June 12. From there unfolded one of the most sensational trials of the 20th century.

Simpson's criminal trial didn't begin until the following January. It lasted more than nine months, generating nearly round-the-clock media coverage and public debate. Even late-night comedians routinely tossed O.J. jokes into their monologues. The prosecution presented mounds of potentially incriminating testimony and physical evidence, none more dramatic than DNA that matched Simpson's blood to that found at the crime scene. His defense was built around accusations of a racially motivated frame-up by the LAPD. The jury, after less than four hours of deliberation, returned a not guilty verdict on October 3, 1995, and Simpson was released from prison.

Nearly three weeks later, Simpson went on trial in a separate civil case resulting from a lawsuit by the victims' families. On January 4, 1996, a jury concluded that he had wrongfully caused the deaths of his ex-wife and Goldman. The court ordered Simpson to pay compensatory damages of $8.5 million and punitive damages of $25 million.

The entire saga provided the public with a vivid portrayal of the justice system and of racial divisions in the country, as well as a glimpse into the future trend of reality television.

for five Stanley Cup titles. In April 1993, highly regarded Mike Keenan (b.1949) signed on to coach the team, which, by the start of the 1993–94 season, featured six members of Messier's championship-rich Oilers' squad. The Rangers compiled the league's best record during the regular season (52-24-8, with 112 points), then advanced to the Stanley Cup Finals against the Vancouver Canucks.

The finals went the distance. Messier came to the rescue in game seven at home in Madison Square Garden, scoring the go-ahead goal. Up 3–2, New York survived a furious third-period attack by Vancouver before wildly celebrating the end of their Stanley Cup drought.

Meanwhile, the Knicks' Agony Continues

Unlike the New York Rangers, with whom they shared Madison Square Garden, the New York Knicks just missed their Garden party when they lost game seven of the NBA Finals to the Houston Rockets on June 22 at The Summit in Houston. It would have been the Knicks' first title since 1973.

Seven-foot centers Patrick Ewing of the Knicks and Hakeem Olajuwon were certainly the centers of attention in this rough-and-tumble defensive battle, in which neither team scored more than 93 points in any of the seven games. Even so, it was the play of guards Sam Cassell of Houston and John Starks of the Knicks that ultimately made the difference.

With the series tied at one game apiece, Cassell scored seven points in the final seconds of game three in New

York to preserve a 93–89 Rockets win. The Knicks won the next two and hoped to finish things off in game six in Houston. Starks, pouring in 27 points, nearly made it happen. But he came up just short in two critical possessions in the closing moments, including a 25-footer blocked by Olajuwon with two seconds left and New York down 86–84.

Starks went ice cold in game seven—2 for 18, including 0 for 11 from three-point range. The Rockets won 90–84 and landed their first NBA championship.

The World Cup Runneth Over

Imagine if Major League Baseball held the World Series in Britain. America's national pastime in a country where the game of cricket is far more popular? It could never happen!

But when FIFA, the international organization that governs soccer, announced that the 1994 World Cup Tournament would be staged in the United States, skeptics wondered what it was thinking. Soccer's grandest event—so special that it is only held every four years—in a country where only little kids play the sport?

Well, not only did the U.S. host the 15th World Cup from June 17 to July 17, but it was also a huge success. Teams from 24 nations played a total of 52 games in arenas across the country, including Giants Stadium in East Rutherford, New Jersey, Soldier Field in Chicago, the Cotton Bowl in Dallas, and the Rose Bowl in Pasadena, California. Nearly 3.5 million fans turned out, while a television audience of more than 35 million tuned in.

Youth soccer is tremendously popular in the United States, and high school and college soccer are growing. Still, the U.S. national team has never been a powerhouse. So it was shocking when the United States upset title contender Colombia, 2–1, in the first round before a crowd of 93,194 at the Rose Bowl on June 22. Indeed, it was the first win in World Cup play for the United States since beating England in 1950.

The United States advanced to the Round of 16, where it was beaten by

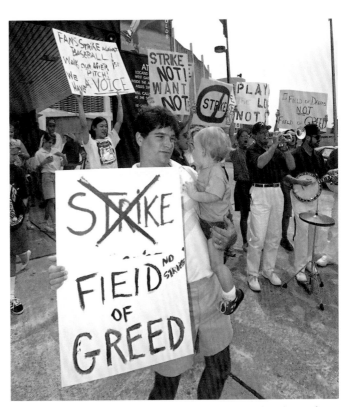

Baseball Strikes Out *Fans were upset with both sides in the labor dispute between owners and players that wiped out much of the 1994 baseball season—including the World Series (see page 48).*

1994

Brazil on July 4 at Stanford Stadium in Stanford, California. Brazil moved on to the finals against Italy on July 17 at the Rose Bowl. The game ended in a tie and had to be decided on a shootout, in which each team alternates in taking five individual shots against the goalie. Brazil won the shootout, 3–2, and the World Cup.

Baseball Strikes Out

For the eighth time since 1972, baseball suffered a work stoppage. And this time, the unthinkable happened: The World Series was cancelled.

On August 12, the players went on strike. As usual, the main issue was money. This time the owners wanted to institute a cap on salaries, limiting how much teams could spend on their total player payroll—something the players' union strongly opposed.

For the next 34 days, fans kept their fingers crossed that the two sides would come to an agreement and resume one of the best seasons in years. Instead, on September 14, acting Commissioner Bud Selig announced that the remainder of the season was cancelled, including the playoffs and the World Series. The strike did not end until March 31, 1995. In those 232 days, 920 games were missed.

In a League of His Own

On September 5, the San Francisco 49ers' Jerry Rice left little doubt that he was the best wide receiver in the history of the NFL. In a 44–14 wipeout of the Los Angeles Raiders on *Monday Night Football*, he caught three touchdown passes. The last one established an NFL record, pushing him one touchdown past legendary Cleveland Browns fullback Jim Brown for a career total of 127.

Jerry Lee Rice was born on October 13, 1962, in Crawford, Mississippi, where he became a high school star in football, basketball, and track. During four seasons at Mississippi Valley State University (1980–1984), Rice set 18 NCAA Division I-AA records. In his senior year alone, the consensus All-American racked up 1,845 yards and scored 28 touchdowns.

The 49ers traded up for the 16th spot in the 1985 NFL draft specifically to land

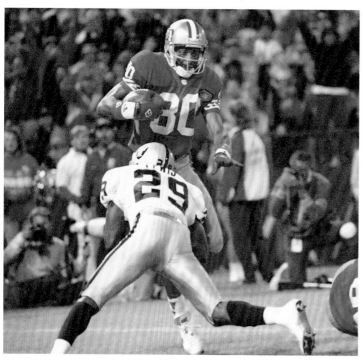

San Francisco Treat *Prolific wide receiver Jerry Rice was still going strong in his 10th NFL season in 1994, when he became the NFL's all-time leading touchdown scorer.*

Other Milestones of 1994

✔ With a famous Arkansan, President Bill Clinton, in attendance at the Charlotte Coliseum in North Carolina, the University of Arkansas beat Duke, 76–72, to claim the NCAA basketball championship on April 4.

✔ Also on April 4, the Chicago Cubs' Tuffy Rhodes became the first player to homer his first three times up on Opening Day (in a 12–8 loss to the Mets).

✔ Sprinter Leroy Burrell set a new world record (9.85 seconds) in the 100-meter sprint on July 6 in Lausanne, Switzerland.

✔ On July 28, Texas Rangers baseball pitcher Kenny Rogers threw a perfect game (no hits, no walks, no runs, and no players to reach first base), blanking the California Angels, 4–0.

✔ After rallying from six holes back, Tiger Woods, at age 18, became the youngest winner of the U.S. Amateur Golf Championship on August 28.

✔ On September 11, Andre Agassi beat Germany's Michael Stich in straight sets to become the first unseeded player to win the men's U.S. Open tennis title since 1966.

Andre Agassi

Rice. The rookie wide receiver scored his first touchdown on a 25-yard pass from quarterback Joe Montana on October 6, 1985, and he just got better from there.

Rice played 16 seasons with the 49ers, then four more years with the Oakland Raiders and Seattle Seahawks. He made the Pro Bowl 13 times, played on three Super Bowl-winning teams, and shattered virtually every receiving record there is, including receptions (1,549), receiving yards (22,895), and touchdowns (197). He finished with 207 total touchdowns, another record. In 2010, Rice was inducted into the Pro Football Hall of Fame.

Tar Heels' Dynasty Sticks

The University of North Carolina's women's soccer team won its ninth straight NCAA title on November 20 in Portland, Oregon, shutting out Notre Dame, 5–0. When the North Carolina Tar Heels won their first title, in 1982, there were only 25 women's teams competing on the NCAA Division I level in soccer. In 1994 there were 154, including 24 in the tournament. That was certainly evidence of soccer's growth in the United States, but more so of UNC's utter dominance of the sport.

1995

49ers Mine More Gold

Quarterback Steve Young passed for a record six touchdowns to lead the San Francisco 49ers to a 49–26 rout of the San Diego Chargers in Super Bowl XXIX at Joe Robbie Stadium on January 29. The 49ers became the first team to win five Super Bowls, and made it 11 consecutive wins for NFC teams over AFC teams in the league title game.

The 49ers' first four Super Bowl wins came in the 1980s. Quarterback extraordinaire Joe Montana was the catalyst for their Super Bowl wins during that decade. But in 1993, Montana was traded to the Kansas City Chiefs, leaving Steve Young (b.1961) to fill some big shoes.

Montana had made a career of throwing the ball to All-Pro wide receiver Jerry Rice (see page 48), and Young-to-Rice certainly sounded strange. Yet it produced similarly spectacular results. The new tandem connected on 112 passes for 1,499 yards and 13 touchdowns during the regular season. And that was just a tune-up for the Super Bowl.

San Francisco's biggest postseason challenge was a Dallas Cowboys' team on a quest for its third straight NFL champi-onship. The 49ers got past the Cowboys on November 13, and again two months later in the NFC Championship Game.

That matchup turned out to be the season's pivotal game because the Super Bowl was yet another blowout. Young and Rice teamed on a touchdown pass on the third play of the game, and the 49ers never looked back.

Rice finished with 10 catches for 149 yards and three touchdowns in all, but the game's MVP was Young. He completed 24 of 36 passes for 325 yards. After the game, 49ers head coach George Seifert—who himself knew about replacing a legend after taking over for Bill Walsh in 1989—called Young one of the greatest quarterbacks in league history. "Joe Montana established a standard," he said, "and Steve Young has maintained it."

Twice Is Nice for Marlin

For a NASCAR driver, winning the Daytona 500 is a dream come true. Winning stock-car racing's most prestigious event two years in a row is almost unheard of. But 37-year-old Sterling Marlin joined an elite group of back-to-back Daytona 500 winners when he held off

High Five *The San Francisco 49ers, led by a record-setting performance from quarterback Steve Young (8), beat the San Diego Chargers in Super Bowl XXIX and became the first team to win the NFL's biggest game five times.*

Dale Earnhardt to win the Daytona International Speedway on February 19.

Marlin had never won any NASCAR race before taking the checkered flag at Daytona in 1994 in his 279th career start. When he won again this year, he joined Richard Petty and Cale Yarborough as the only drivers to win the race in back-to-back seasons. He also became the first—and still only—driver to make the Daytona 500 his first two career victories.

In all, Marlin has won 10 races in a career that still included a limited schedule of events in 2009.

He's Ba-a-a-a-ack!

You're the best basketball player on the planet, so why quit to take up baseball? That question probably crossed Michael Jordan's mind during his 17-month hiatus from the NBA. So after a season of Minor League Baseball, the former outfielder rejoined the Chicago Bulls on March 19.

In his first game back, against the Indiana Pacers—and wearing his baseball number 45 instead of his familiar 23—Jordan scored 19 points.

This Girl's Got Game *Forward Rebecca Lobo and the University of Connecticut soared to the NCAA women's basketball title with a 35-0 record. UConn vanquished University of Tennessee in the title game.*

38-point effort in game two in the next round of the playoffs, against Shaquille O'Neal (b.1972) and the Orlando Magic, the Bulls lost the series in six games.

"We weren't the same team we were 18 months ago," Jordan admitted in the post-game press conference, "but the fun part is trying to live up to the accomplishments of the past."

Perfectly Done

The University of Connecticut's women's basketball team did more than win the NCAA Division I Championship on April 2, defeating the University of Tennessee, 70–64. They even did more than complete the season with a perfect 35–0 record. The Lady Huskies put women's college basketball on the map.

Not that women didn't already have game. Superstars such as Cheryl Miller and Sheryl Swoopes had paved the way at the University of Southern California and Texas Tech University, respectively. And Tennessee's Pat Summit, with 564 wins by season's end, was one of the nation's most accomplished head coaches, man or woman. This UConn squad, though, took the game to a new level.

The poster girl was Rebecca Lobo (b.1973), a 6-foot-4 forward with a great perimeter game and a 4.0 grade-point average—an amazing role model to legions of girls. She and the Huskies earned the number-one ranking in January after knocking off Tennessee, and they never looked back. In the title game, at the Target Center in Minneapolis, Lobo got into foul trouble in the first half, which helped Tennessee's Lady Vols to a 38–32 halftime

If there was any rust on the 32-year-old Jordan's game, he shook it off against his old rival, the New York Knicks. On March 28, he set a Madison Square Garden record with 55 points in a 113–111 Bulls' squeaker. He looked pretty much his old self in leading Chicago to a first-round victory in the playoffs against the Charlotte Hornets, averaging 31.5 points in four games. Yet, despite Jordan's vintage advantage. Lobo and point guard Jennifer Rizzotti led the charge back, though, and UConn completed its dream season in perfect fashion.

They're Ba-a-a-a-a-ack!

Major League Baseball returned from its longest work stoppage on April 25. The shortened season—144 games instead of the normal 162—produced enough goodwill to begin winning back the hearts of disgruntled fans. .

The Cleveland Indians, long the doormats of the American League, finished with 100 wins for the first time since 1954. The Seattle Mariners reached the postseason for the first time in team history. Their thrilling, extra-innings victory in game five of the division series in September against the New York Yankees, who hadn't won anything since 1981, lifted them to the American League Championship Series (ALCS). Although the Mariners fell to the Indians, who won the best-of-seven ALCS in six games, the run probably saved baseball in Seattle.

The Colorado Rockies, in just their third season, made the playoffs, but lost to the pitching-rich Atlanta Braves (ace Greg Maddux, thanks to a 19–2 record and a skimpy 1.63 ERA, won his unprecedented fourth straight Cy Young Award). The Braves then swept the Cincinnati Reds and faced the Indians in a World Series in October that confirmed the old saying that good pitching beats good hitting.

As a team, the Indians hit .291 for the season—the best in Major League Baseball. Their lineup featured Albert Belle, who rang up 50 home runs, and veteran Eddie Murray, who whacked his 3,000th career hit on June 30. The Braves' pitching staff had the lowest ERA, at 3.44, in the major leagues.

Maddux opened the Series with a two-hit gem in which he pitched all nine innings; only four balls left the infield. Down two games to none, the Indians won two of three games at home. In game six back in Atlanta, Tom Glavine pitched eight innings and gave up just one hit, David Justice smacked a sixth-inning homer, and closing pitcher Mark Wohlers threw a perfect ninth inning to seal the 1–0 Braves' win. It marked the team's return to baseball's mountaintop after a 37-year absence—and baseball's return to the hearts of its fans.

The Nation Mourns

On April 23, audiences at sports arenas, stadiums, and ballparks across the country observed a moment of silence to honor the victims of what was then the worst terrorist attack ever in the United States. On the morning of April 19, a massive bomb hidden inside a rental truck exploded in front of the Alfred P. Murrah Federal Building in Oklahoma City, killing 168 men, women, and children. Just 90 minutes later, an Oklahoma Highway Patrol officer pulled over 27-year-old Timothy McVeigh for driving without a license plate. Shortly before he was to be released on April 21, McVeigh, an Army veteran, was recognized as a bombing suspect and was charged with the deadly crime. Not long after, an ex-Army friend of McVeigh's, Terry Nichols, was also arrested and charged. The men were tried in two separate, emotional, and highly publicized trials. In June 1997, a jury convicted McVeigh and sentenced him to death. He was executed on June 11, 2001. Nichols was found guilty of involuntary manslaughter and of conspiring with McVeigh. He was sentenced to life in prison.

Baseball's New Iron Man

New York Yankees legend Lou Gehrig (1903–1941) earned the nickname "The Iron Horse" after playing in 2,130 consecutive games. That seemingly insurmountable record was eclipsed at Baltimore's Camden Yards on September 6 in what proved to be baseball's greatest welcome-back gift back to strike-weary fans. On that festive summer evening, Baltimore Orioles shortstop Cal Ripken Jr. (b.1960) played in his 2,131st straight game.

Once the fifth inning of the contest against the California Angels was complete and the game became official, Ripken ran a victory lap around the stadium, stopping and shaking hands with fans and players. The scoreboard read, "Cal, thank you for saving baseball." During a 22-minute, 15-second ovation, Ripken received eight curtain calls from the appreciative crowd.

"I know that if Lou Gehrig is looking down on tonight's activities," he told the throng, "he isn't concerned about someone playing one more consecutive game than he did. Instead, he's viewing tonight as just another example of what is good and right about the great American game."

Ripken began his iron man streak on May 30, 1982, and played in 19,231 out of a possible 19,395

innings. And he went all-out in every single one. Even in this most special of games, he homered to help boost the Orioles to a 4–2 win.

A local boy, born on August 24, 1960, in nearby Havre de Grace, Ripken earned AL Rookie of the Year honors in 1982 and was twice named the league's MVP (1983 and 1991). He started in 17 straight All-Star Games beginning in 1984 (the last three as a third baseman), and hit more home runs than any other shortstop (402).

At 6-foot-4, Ripken was the tallest full-time shortstop, and he set the single-season fielding percentage (a measure of defensive success calculated by dividing the number of successful plays a fielder makes by the total chances he has to play the ball) at the position (.996 in 1990). He recorded the final putout in the 1983 World Series, when the Orioles defeated the Philadelphia Phillies in five games for their first championship since 1970.

Cal Ripken Jr.

Ripken ended his streak at 2,632 games by taking himself out of the lineup on September 20, 1998. He retired at the end of the 2001 season with a lifetime batting average of .297 in 3,001 games. Next stop: the Baseball Hall of Fame.

Rockets-Powered Sweep

The Houston Rockets swept the Orlando Magic in four games to repeat as NBA champions. While some liked to believe their 1994 title had a lot to do with a Chicago Bulls team that no longer had Michael Jordan, the Rockets put that notion to rest. In fact, after the 113–101 game four on June 14 in Houston, the Rockets became the first team in NBA history to defeat four 50-win teams on the way to a championship.

Before sweeping the Magic, they put away, in order, the Utah Jazz, the Phoenix Suns, and the San Antonio Spurs. And in none of those series did the Rockets have home-court advantage.

X Marks the Sport

The amateur athletes of Generation X (those born between 1965 and 1975) explored new sporting thrills in the 1990s. Shunning tradition, they pioneered alternative sports such as inline skating, snowboarding, mountain biking, and street luge.

ESPN, the all-sports cable channel, quickly saw the potential and seized on a programming opportunity to appeal to a key audience by launching the Extreme Games. Held June 24 to July 1 in Rhode Island and Vermont, the inaugural games featured 27 events, including bungee jumping, barefoot waterski jumping, kite skiing, windsurfing, sky surfing, and bicycle stunt riding.

Not only was the competition gnarly, but it also proved a ratings hit with the all-important group of male TV viewers aged 12 to 34 that advertisers covet. So it was a no-brainer for ESPN to capitalize on the extreme theme every year.

ESPN added a winter version in 1996 and shortened the name to X Games. The snow and ice edition featured such extreme sports as snowboarding, ice climbing, and super-modified shovel racing. Continued success and popularity eventually made the X Games a prime-time event for a new generation of international athletes and TV audiences for years to come. In 2010, ESPN held the Winter X Games 14 and the Summer X Games 16.

X Marks the Spot *ESPN cornered a coveted demographic with the introduction of the Extreme Games. The X Games, as they soon were called, quickly grew in stature and popularity.*

55

1995

NBC Locks Up Olympics

NBC announced on December 12 that it had purchased the rights to televise each Winter and Summer Olympic Games through 2008 for $2.3 billion.

The roots for that astounding total date to 1960, the year that Americans got their first look at the Olympics on television. That year, CBS paid the International Olympic Committee $50,000 to air 15 hours of the Winter Games from Squaw Valley, California. On August 7, 1995, NBC paid a whopping $1.25 billion for the U.S. rights to broadcast the 2000 Summer Games from Sydney, Australia,

as well as the Winter Games from Salt Lake City, Utah, two years later.

Securing the television rights to sporting events had become a highly competitive business. Viewers never seemed to get enough sports—consider the popularity of cable channel ESPN—and advertisers wanted to reach those audiences. So the networks battled one another and paid millions to air baseball, football, and basketball. (As one example, on November 6, Major League Baseball announced a five-year, $1.7 billion deal with NBC, ESPN, Fox, and Prime Liberty Cable.)

The Olympics, now alternating every two years between Summer and Winter Games (see page 30), generated huge

Other Milestones of 1995

✔ On January 6, Atlanta Hawks coach Lenny Wilkens notched career win No. 939—a 112–90 defeat of the Washington Bullets—to become the NBA's all-time winningest coach, surpassing the Boston Celtics' Red Auerbach.

✔ Doug Swingley and his nine-dog team finished the Iditarod Trail Sled Dog Race across Alaska on March 14 in record time, completing the 1,160-mile course in nine days, two hours, 42 minutes, 19 seconds.

✔ On June 30, the Cleveland Indians' Eddie Murray collected hit No. 3,000 of his big-league career in a game against the Minnesota Twins.

Doug Swingley and team

✔ On June 24, the New Jersey Devils completed their four-game sweep of the Detroit Red Wings to win the NHL's Stanley Cup.

✔ By defeating German Boris Becker on July 9, Pete Sampras became the first U.S. male tennis player to win three consecutive Wimbledon championships.

✔ Dan Marino, quarterback of the Miami Dolphins, completed career pass number 3,687 in a 27–24 loss to the Indianapolis Colts to set an NFL record. He retired in 1999 also holding career records for completions, yards, and touchdowns.

prime-time television ratings for two weeks. Although the networks didn't necessarily make money broadcasting them because the expenses involved in covering them were so high, they benefited from the prestige and the opportunity to promote their other programming.

ABC had dominated Olympics broadcasting through the 1980s, and NBC landing the Sydney and Salt Lake Games was considered a coup. The deal involved two rounds of international dealing by NBC Sports president Dick Ebersol. It began with a secret New York-to-Sweden-to-Montreal-to-New York trip in early August, during which he outfoxed Fox Network owner Rupert Murdoch, who had offered the IOC $701 million for the Sydney rights. Ebersol upped the ante to $705 million, and in an unusual move, he got the Salt Lake Games for an extra $545 million—marking the first time the IOC had sold more than one Olympics at a time. Four months later, on December 12, in an even more-stunning move, NBC announced that it had secured the rights to every Summer and Winter Games through 2008 for $2.3 billion.

The Glass Slipper Fits

Who knows how Cinderella came to be associated with sports teams? But there seems to be one or two Cinderella stories every year—teams relegated to the dust pile who unexpectedly out-shine the competition. In 1995, the role fell to the Northwestern University Wildcats football team. For ages a perennial loser in the Big Ten Conference, Northwestern enjoyed one of those when-you-wish-upon-a-star seasons.

It started on September 2 in South Bend, Indiana, when the Wildcats stunned the Notre Dame Fighting Irish, 17–15. Northwestern, a 28-point underdog, had last beaten the Irish in 1962. On October 7, the Wildcats marched into Ann Arbor and upset the University of Michigan Wolverines, 19–13. A week later, they magically made the University of Wisconsin's Badgers disappear, 35–0! On November 4, the sixth-ranked Wildcats hosted number-12 Penn State University and tamed the Nittany Lions, 21–10. In that game, Northwestern running back Darnell Autry gained 100 yards in his 10th straight game, set a school season rushing record, and scored three touchdowns.

When Michigan spoiled previously unbeaten and second-ranked Ohio State University's hopes of winning the Big Ten by upending the Buckeyes on November 25, Northwestern grabbed the conference title. They were off to the big ball, the Rose Bowl, for the first time since 1947, against the 17th-ranked University of Southern California Trojans.

Alas, the clock struck midnight on New Year's Day, 1996, in Pasadena, California, where Northwestern's storybook season ended with a 41–32 loss.

1996

Brown Out

The Cleveland Browns long have had some of the most rabid fans in football. Their stadium even has a famous section of fans called the "Dawg Pound." But those loyal followers were left without a team when NFL owners approved the move of the Browns to Baltimore on February 8—well, sort of.

Baltimore indeed would get a new team, called the Ravens, who would take the Browns' place in the AFC's Central Division. And that team would have most of the Browns' old players. But technically, the NFL considered the Ravens a brand new team. Cleveland got to keep the Browns' team name, logos, and history, which dated to 1946, when the team was part of the All-America Football Conference. That wasn't much consolation to the fans, though, who didn't have a team to root for until the new Cleveland Browns were formed in 1999.

Michigan Melts the Ice

College hockey typically has a tough time grabbing the headlines from football and basketball. Not so at the University of Michigan in the early 1990s. From 1993 to 1995, the Michigan Wolverines played to a 93–22–5 record. And when the team scored the winning goal in overtime to seal the 1996 NCAA championship against Colorado College on March 30, it generated even bigger news, because the Wolverines' hopes of skating to a national title had melted away in each of the last three NCAA hockey playoffs—all heartbreaking overtime losses.

The school had been a hockey powerhouse in the 1950s, winning five championships in six years from 1951 to 1956. But its last title had come 32 years ago. So when the 1996 Wolverines faced yet another overtime, in front of a crowd of 13,330 at Riverfront Coliseum in Cincinnati, they hoped recent history would not repeat itself.

At 3:35 into the overtime period, Brendan Morrison, a two-time All-America forward, rebounded a missed shot and fired the puck into the Colorado net. Final score: Michigan 3, Colorado 2.

"We needed this for people to understand just how successful this program is," said Michigan coach Red Berenson. "Winning a national championship isn't easy."

Tiny Athlete, Big Heart *Injured Kerri Strug came to the victory stand in the arms of her coach, Bela Karolyi, after the U.S. women struck gymnastics gold (see page 60).*

Unbelieva-Bulls

Any doubts about Michael Jordan's worth to the Chicago Bulls were laid to rest during the 1995–1996 NBA season. With all due respect to Scottie Pippen, Toni Kukoc, Dennis Rodman, and the rest of the Bulls, they simply weren't the same team without Jordan. Not even close.

Jordan turned 33 in February, and age and the 17-month fling with baseball forced him to alter his game. His gravity-defying dunks went down less frequently, but refinement of a fade-away jump shot and career-best accuracy from three-point range (.427) more than made up for it. Jordan led the NBA in scoring (at 30.4 points per game) for a record eighth time in his career and won his fourth league MVP award.

As great as the Bulls were before Jordan left the first time (see page 37),

1996

this edition rewrote the record books. On February 27, with a 120–99 taming of the Minnesota Timberwolves, Chicago became the quickest team in North American professional sports history to reach 50 wins in a season. A come-from-behind victory over the Milwaukee Bucks on April 16 made the Bulls the first NBA team to achieve 70 wins; they finished the regular season at 72–10.

Chicago lost only one game in the first three rounds of the playoffs. Then, in the NBA Finals, the Bulls eliminated the Seattle SuperSonics in six games. The MVP of the best-of-seven championship series? Jordan, of course.

Jordan's greatness might seem almost robotic, yet he demonstrated very human emotion after the final buzzer sounded on June 16 at the United Center in Chicago. As the sold-out crowd cheered another NBA title, he grabbed the game ball and dashed to the Bulls' locker room. This was Jordan's first championship without his late father there to join in the celebration. Overcome with lingering grief, he lay on the floor in tears, clutching the basketball—on Father's Day.

The Atlanta Olympics

Boxing legend Muhammad Ali lit the torch at the Opening Ceremony to officially kick off the XXVI Summer Olympic Games in Atlanta on July 19. Ali, a gold medalist at the 1960 Games in Rome and now a beloved figure worldwide, provided ideal illumination for the brilliant athletic achievements to come over the next two weeks. Although the Games were marred by a bomb at an

Atlanta park on July 27 that left one person dead and 100 injured, and complaints of over-commercialization dogged local organizers, these Olympics were otherwise a success.

As with any Olympics, stories aplenty preceded the competition. Among the most compelling was speculation over whether American sprinter Michael Johnson (b.1967) would become the first male Olympian to win both the 200-meter and 400-meter races. He had already pulled off the double at the 1995 world championships, and track and field officials changed the Olympic schedule so he could attempt it again in Atlanta.

Johnson had "owned" the 400-meter event since 1989, winning 54 straight finals. But before the 1992 Olympics in Barcelona, Spain, he contracted a severe case of food poisoning that prevented him from competing. This time, he would not be denied. On July 29, he cruised to the gold medal, crossing the finish line with the largest margin of victory in the event in 10 years.

Two days later, Johnson made Olympic history in shimmering style. Wearing gold-colored running shoes, he stumbled slightly coming out of the starting blocks, but quickly recovered. Johnson already held the world record in the 200-meter race—set at 19.66 seconds in June—and when he kicked into hyperspeed about halfway through this race, he established an astonishing new mark of 19.32.

Gail Devers provided one of the most inspirational stories in Atlanta. A world-class sprinter and hurdler, she had overcome a serious thyroid disorder called Graves Disease, that sidelined her for two years (1989 to 1990) and nearly resulted in having both feet amputated. She not only returned to competition, but won the 100-meter sprint at the 1992 Olympics in a photo finish. At these Games, the same thing happened. Although Devers and Jamaica's Christine Ottey finished with identical times in the 100-meters, the judges declared Devers the gold medalist by the smallest of margins—an infinitesimal two centimeters.

At age 35, Carl Lewis, who had already won eight Olympic gold medals, took an unexpected ninth on July 29. He had won the long jump at the previous three Olympics, but he was not considered a contender this time. Nonetheless, on his third jump in the finals, he leaped into first place and then watched anxiously as the competition failed to beat him.

Americans captured a total of 44 gold medals in Atlanta, though none more heroically than in the team competition in women's gymnastics. The event combines the scores of each team's five athletes on the required apparatus (vault, uneven bars, balance beam, floor exercise). The U.S. team held a slight lead over the Russians as the United States competed on its last apparatus, the vault.

When the teammate before her faltered, 18-year-old Kerri Strug figured the gold depended on her performance. On her first attempt, she fell. Worse than that, she heard a sickening snap in her left ankle. That wasn't going to stop her, though. In excruciating pain and at the urging of her team, coach, and cheering spectators, Strug landed her next vault perfectly—then collapsed in agony. She had to be carried to the medal stand by her coach with a cast around her severely sprained ankle, as the gold medal was hung around her neck. Only later did Strug realize that the team would have won anyway, but that hardly diminished her gutsy feat.

Gymnastics wasn't the only sport in which a U.S. women's team achieved greatness. While the men's more-heralded Dream Team III breezed to the gold in basketball, the women hoopsters proved

MLS Kicks Off

Spurred by the popularity of the 1994 World Cup in America, soccer grew in stature in the decade, culminating with the launch of a new 10-team professional league, Major League Soccer, on April 6. Before a crowd of 31,683 at Spartan Stadium in San Jose, California, the hometown Clash outlasted Washington D.C. United, 1–0.

Fears that the league would fail, as several past attempts in the U.S. had, were soon put to rest when the Los Angeles Galaxy home opener against the New York/New Jersey MetroStars drew 69,255 to the Rose Bowl. For the 16-game season, the MLS attracted 2,786,673 fans, for a respectable average of 17,416 per contest—well over the projected 12,000 figure.

The MLS Cup championship game, on October 20 in front of 34,643 fans at rain-soaked, windswept Foxboro (Massachusetts) Stadium and a national TV audience, provided a thrilling climax to the inaugural season. The Galaxy and D.C. United played to a 2–2 tie at the end of regulation time. A little more than three minutes into the sudden-death overtime, D.C. United's Eddie Pope headed a corner kick for the winning goal. "Soccer fever is alive in the United States," said a jubilant D.C. United captain John Harkes during the post-game revelry, "and it's here to stay."

King of Swing

Pete Sampras dominated men's tennis during the 1990s. He burst onto the scene at the 1990 U.S. Open, one of the sport's four annual Grand Slam tournaments (the others are the Australian Open, the French Open, and Wimbledon). At 19 years, 28 days, he became the Open's youngest male winner, after dispensing with Ivan Lendl, John McEnroe, and Andre Agassi in the last three rounds. Sampras powered his way to 11 more Grand Slam titles during the decade, though perhaps none more memorable than back at the U.S. Open in 1996.

Born on August 12, 1971, in Washington, D.C., Sampras began playing tennis at age seven. He turned professional at 16 in 1988, won his first pro tournament in February 1990, and achieved the number-one ranking for the first of many times in April 1993. By the time he arrived back at the U.S. Open site at the

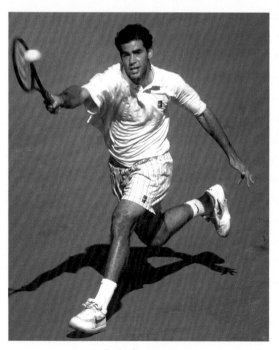

Pete Sampras

National Tennis Center in Flushing, New York, for the 1996 event, Sampras had already won a half dozen more Grand Slam tournaments, including three straight Wimbledon titles (1993–1995). He also arrived with a heavy heart.

Tim Gullikson, Sampras' longtime coach, mentor, and close friend, had died of brain cancer in May. All year, a grieving Sampras had a hard time concentrating on his game. For the first time since 1992, he failed to win a Grand Slam. Then, on September 5 in the U.S. Open quarterfinal against 22-year-old Spaniard Alex Corretja, he played one of the most inspired matches in the history of the tournament. It went five sets and lasted four hours, nine minutes. Suffering from stomach cramps, Sampras vomited twice during the final set. Barely able to stand, much less serve and volley, he summoned up the energy to defeat Corretja. Three days later—on what would have been Gullikson's 45th birthday—Sampras beat Michael Chang for the title. "I've been thinking about him [Gullikson] all day and all during the match, about things he told me," Sampras said in the post-match press conference. "I still feel his spirit. He is still very much in my heart."

Sampras continued his masterful play over the remainder of the decade, winning four more Grand Slam titles. He also retained his number-one ranking, which he'd held since 1993, for a record six consecutive years, until 1998. (Sampras played through 2002 and finished with a then-record 14 career Grand Slam singles titles.)

After losing to him in the Wimbledon final in 1999, Agassi was asked by the Associated Press whether Sampras was the greatest player ever. Agassi did not hesitate. "Yes," he said. "He's accomplished more than anybody else has, in my opinion. No question about it. His achievements speak for themselves."

equally impressive. Undefeated in their yearlong pre-Olympic tour (52–0), they won all eight of their games in Atlanta, culminating with a convincing 111–87 victory over Brazil in the gold-medal match-up. The women's soccer team finished 4–0–1 in the first Olympic soccer tournament, including a riveting 2–1 win over China for the gold medal. The U.S. women also beat a strong Chinese team in the inaugural softball tournament final, 3–1. Dr. Dot Richardson, the team's 34-year-old shortstop and an orthopedic surgeon, made the difference with a two-run homer. Several controversial calls against the Chinese led to protests, but video reviews proved the umpires were correct.

American women were golden in the swimming pool, too. Leading the way was the surprising 23-year-old Amy Van Dyken (b. 1973), whose childhood asthma was so bad, she used to collapse just walking up a flight of stairs.

Van Dyken took up swimming to increase her lung capacity, and by high school was a state champion. Her lungs worked just fine in Atlanta. She took individual golds in the 50-meter freestyle and 100-meter butterfly, and was a member of the U.S. teams that won the 4-by-100-meter freestyle and 4-by-100 medley relays.

Van Dyken thus became the first American woman to win four gold medals in one Olympic Games, either Summer or Winter. Teammate Jenny Thompson (b. 1973), who brought home two relay gold medals from the 1992 Olympic Games in Barcelona, Spain, picked up three more gold medals in the relays in Atlanta.

Tiger's Tale Grows

He was only two years old when he appeared on television's *Mike Douglas Show*, hitting golf balls with ageless comedian Bob Hope. The knee-high golf prodigy shot a 48 for nine holes at age three and was featured in *Golf Digest* magazine at age five. By 1996, Eldrick "Tiger" Woods (b.1975) had established himself as an emerging star. On August 25, he won an unprecedented third straight U.S. Amateur golf title in a spectacular fashion that would follow him into his record-setting professional career.

At Pumpkin Ridge Golf Club in North Plains, Oregon, Woods found himself five strokes down halfway through the 36-hole final match against University of Florida ace Steve Scott. The Tiger clawed his way back to a tie at the end of regulation play, then clinched his historic title on the second extra hole. The comeback capped a phenomenal amateur career in which he won three U.S. Junior Amateur championships. In two years at Stanford University (1995–1996), he won 10 collegiate events, including the NCAA golf title in 1996.

Two days after his smashing performance at Pumpkin Ridge, Woods turned pro by joining the Professional Golfers Association (PGA) tour at the Greater Milwaukee Open. He finished tied for 60th place, but more important, he made his much-anticipated professional debut (he had played in numerous pro tournaments since 1992, including the Masters and the U.S. Open, but with amateur status). The public had become fascinated not just with his amazing game, but also

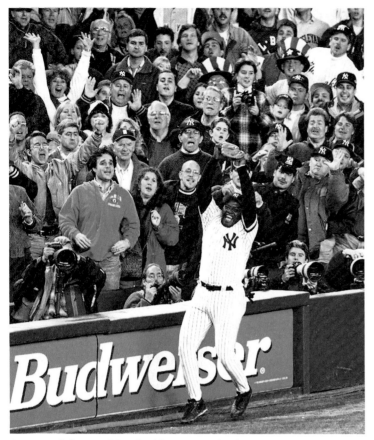

On Top of the World *Third baseman Charlie Hayes and New York Yankees' fans celebrate the final out of the 1996 World Series. New York beat Atlanta in six games for its first title since 1978.*

off to capture the Las Vegas Invitational. Two weeks later, at the Walt Disney World/ Oldsmobile Classic in Orlando, he edged Payne Stewart for his second pro victory. Woods earned $940,420 in 11 tournaments worldwide and signed endorsement deals with Nike and Titleist worth $60 million. He was named the PGA Rookie of the Year and *Sports Illustrated's* Sportsman of the Year.

Sports Illustrated managing editor Bill Colson wrote an editorial explaining the choice of Woods over other remarkable athletes of 1996: "It seems clear, to us anyway, that one young man has recently surpassed all the others—perhaps in deeds but certainly in the long ripples those deeds produced. Tiger Woods, all of 20, all of four months as a pro under his belt after he won, in most dramatic fashion, a remarkable third straight U.S. Amateur title, is the only one among the candidates who changed the face of a sport, perhaps more rapidly than any other athlete ever has. In case you blinked and missed it, golf is no longer your father's sport."

Yanks End Slumber

The New York Yankees held off the Atlanta Braves 3–2 at Yankee Stadium on October 26 to win the World Series four games to two. The victory was the Yankees' record 23rd in the Fall Classic, but it marked their first title since 1978. The 18 years between World Series wins was the longest since New York won its first title in 1923.

Under new manager Joe Torre (b.1940), the Yankees finished the regular season in first place (92–70), then beat the

his ethnicity. Woods' father was African-American, his mother is from Thailand. In a predominantly white sport, Woods was being compared to the late, great Jackie Robinson, who broke baseball's color barrier in 1947.

Woods, while confident in his abilities and aspirations, tried to downplay the race issue. "I'm not out just to be the best black player," he said. "I want to be the best golfer ever."

Before the year ended, Woods won two PGA events. On October 6, he held off Davis Love III in a sudden-death play-

Texas Rangers and the Baltimore Orioles in the playoffs to reach the World Series.

Meanwhile, in the National League, the Atlanta Braves maintained their supremacy by wrapping up their fifth N.L. East title in the last six years (96–66). They beat the Los Angeles Dodgers and St. Louis Cardinals in the N.L. playoffs to reach the Fall Classic.

The Braves burst into Yankee Stadium on October 20 on a roll. They stunned their hosts 12–1 in game one, and, after Atlanta shut out the Yankees 4–0 in game two—behind an 82-pitch, eight-inning gem from Greg Maddux—many wondered if New York was outmatched. Not quite, as the Yankees won three straight games in Atlanta. The Series took a dramatic turn in game four when New York battled back from a 6–0 deficit; the decisive moment was a three-run homer by Jim Leyritz in the eighth inning to tie the score. The Yanks prevailed, 8–6, in 10 innings.

Game six finally produced a win for the home team, and the Yankees were champs. Said Torre afterward: "Second place is not an option with [owner] George Steinbrenner, which is fine by me."

Other Milestones of 1996

✔ The University of Nebraska, on the heels of a 62–24 pasting of number two University of Florida in the Fiesta Bowl on January 2, became the first college football team in 16 years to win back-to-back national championships.

✔ Don Shula, head coach of the Miami Dolphins since 1970, resigned on January 5. His legacy included an NFL-record 347 wins, two Super Bowl titles (VII and VIII), and the only perfect record (17–0 in 1972) in NFL history.

✔ The Dallas Cowboys beat the Pittsburgh Steelers, 27–17, in Super Bowl XXX on January 28 in Tempe, Arizona. Dallas cornerback Larry Brown earned game MVP honors after setting up 14 second-half points with a pair of interceptions.

Nebraska quarterback Frankie London

✔ The Kentucky Wildcats topped the Syracuse Orangemen, 76–67, to win the NCAA men's basketball championship on April 1. It marked the Wildcats' sixth national title.

✔ In the final round of the Masters golf tournament on April 14, Greg Norman blew a six-shot lead and was overtaken by eventual winner Nick Faldo.

✔ Seattle Mariners shortstop Alex Rodriguez, the top pick in the 1993 draft, hit .358 with 36 home runs and 123 runs batted in, fulfilling the promise many had seen in his play.

✔ Boxer Evander Holyfield scored a surprising 11th-round technical knockout of Mike Tyson to gain the heavyweight title on November 9.

1997

The Pack Is Back

The Green Bay Packers beat the New England Patriots 35–21 in Super Bowl XXXI at the Louisiana Superdome in New Orleans on January 26. The victory was the Packers' first in the Super Bowl since winning games I and II to cap the 1966 and 1967 seasons.

Balance was the hallmark of this 13–3 Packers team. Quarterback Brett Favre (b.1969) won his second straight NFL MVP award after throwing an NFC-record 39 touchdowns to several receivers. Veteran defensive end Reggie White was the bedrock of the defense.

Less than a minute into the second quarter against the 11–5 Patriots, Favre tossed a Super Bowl-record, 81-yard touchdown bomb to Antonio Freeman. The Packers scored another 10 points before halftime. Undaunted, the Patriots crept to within six points on Curtis Martin's 18-yard touchdown run late in the third quarter, but then Green Bay's Desmond Howard snapped their spirit with a 99-yard return of the ensuing kickoff. A two-point conversion capped off the scoring—and the triumphant back-to-Titletown season for the Packers.

Fresh Prince of NASCAR

Jeff Gordon (b.1971) didn't have the Southern pedigree of Richard Petty, the recently retired King of stock car racing (see page 33). But the clean-cut Midwesterner, like Petty, became a royal pain in the neck to his fellow NASCAR competitors.

Gordon got his engine running right at the start of the Winston Cup season, winning the Daytona 500 on February 14. He promised team owner Rick Hendrick, who was back home in North Carolina fighting leukemia, that he'd win the race. Not only did Gordon, at age 25, become the youngest driver to win NASCAR's most prestigious event, but he led a one-two-three sweep of Hendrick-team cars (Terry Labonte and Rickey Craven finished second and third, respectively).

Less fortunate was Dale Earnhardt (1952–2001), who was still looking for his first Daytona win in 19 tries. Gordon passed Earnhardt for second place with 10 laps to go, and the move set in motion a huge crash that left Earnhardt's car a mess. Instead of taking himself out of the race, though, Earnhardt climbed back inside the wreck and finished 31st.

Sunday Drive *Tiger Woods left no doubt he was golf's next superstar with a whopping 12-stroke victory at the prestigious Masters tournament (see page 69).*

Gordon went on to post one of the most remarkable seasons in NASCAR history. He took nine more of the 31 races on the Winston Cup circuit, winning $4,201,227 along the way. Plus, he fin-ished first in two of the other four major races: the Coca-Cola 600 and the Southern 500 (the fourth is the Winston 500). That earned him the Winston Million—a cool $1 million bonus—which had only

Boy Wonder *Twenty-five-year-old Jeff Gordon won his first Daytona 500 in 1997 and went on dominate the NAS-CAR circuit en route to winning driver-of-the-year honors.*

been won once before, by "Million-Dollar" Bill Elliott in 1985. With the princely sum of his season, Gordon was easily crowned Winston Cup driver of the year.

In the 'Zona

The University of Arizona Wildcats finished in just fifth place in the Pacific-10 Conference during the 1996–97 regular season, but head coach Lute Olson's squad hit its stride at just the right time. The Wildcats knocked off three No. 1 seeds en route to winning the NCAA Men's Basketball Tournament, including an 84–79 victory in overtime against Kentucky in the final game March 31 in Indianapolis.

The NCAA tournament featured the usual first-round upsets: number 15 seed Coppin State University surprised second-seeded University of South Carolina; number 14 seed University of Tennessee at Chattanooga upset number three University of Georgia; number 12 seed College of Charleston beat number five University of Maryland. Even so, three of the number-one seeds advanced to the Final Four at the RCA Dome in Indianapolis. The lone exception was Kansas, which dropped an 85–82 decision to Arizona in the Southeast Region semifinals.

In the national semifinals, defending champion Kentucky beat the University of Minnesota for the right to meet Arizona (which defeated North Carolina) two nights later.

Arizona led by one point at halftime, 33–32. With 61 seconds left in the game, Arizona was up 72–68, seemingly on its way to the school's first national basketball championship. But Kentucky's Ron Mercer and Anthony Epps each hit three-pointers; Arizona could only score two more points for the tie, and the game went into overtime. Kentucky lost its earlier momentum in the five-minute extra period and was forced to foul. Arizona kept its cool, sank enough free throws, and prevailed, 84–79. Arizona became the first school ever to knock off three No. 1 seeds in the tournament en route to winning the title.

Arizona and Kentucky both were composed mostly of freshman and sophomores whose relatively raw talent brought them this far. Yet this tournament, wrote Paul Attner in *The Sporting News*, "provided a wonderful road map to show us where the sport is headed after too many years of losing too many elite underclassmen to the NBA."

Tiger Tames Augusta

The golf world had been waiting for this moment, for Tiger Woods to take on the man-eating course at Augusta National Golf Club in Augusta, Georgia. But with his record-setting 12-stroke victory in the annual Masters Tournament, April 10 to 13, it could be an eternity before we see another such masterful performance. The 21-year-old golf genius made Augusta seem like a miniature golf course.

Woods' incredible golfing performance came on what is considered to be among the most challenging courses in the sport. Augusta's long, narrow fairways, treacherous bunkers, and rolling greens have tested and taunted the best players in the game ever since legendary golfer Bobby Jones created the course and the tournament in 1934.

Woods got off to a shaky start in the four-day tournament. He shot 40 on the first nine holes of the 18-hole course, but then settled into a groove. That's an understatement. Over the next three days and 63 holes, he shot 22 under par, finishing 18 under to break the great Jack Nicklaus' (b. 1940) and Ray Floyd's Masters record. His 12-stroke win was the largest margin of victory in a major tournament since Tom Morris won the 1862 British Open by 13 strokes. (Besides the Masters and the British Open, the two other majors are the U.S. Open and the PGA Championship.)

"He's out there playing another game on a golf course he is going to own for a long time," said Nicklaus, who won the Masters at age 23 and whose six titles are more than anyone else's—so far.

A League of Their Own

The eight-team Women's National Basketball Association (WNBA), an affiliate of the NBA, tipped off its inaugural season on June 21 as the New York Liberty beat the Los Angeles Sparks, 67–57. A crowd of 14,284 at the Great Western Forum, in Inglewood, California, witnessed Sparks guard Penny Toler score the first basket in WNBA history.

A hybrid of the pro and college games, the WNBA features a 30-second shot clock, a 19-foot, nine-inch three-point line, two 20-minute halves, 11-player rosters, and a signature orange-and-oatmeal, collegiate-size basketball (28.5 inches in circumference, one inch smaller than the NBA's regulation ball).

The teams, with recent college stars such as Lisa Leslie, Rebecca Lobo, Sheryl Swoopes, and Cynthia Cooper, played 28 games in 1997. On August 30, the Houston Comets, led by league MVP Cooper's

We've Come A Long Way

The other remarkable aspect of Tiger Woods' phenomenal win at Augusta had to do with his ethnicity (half African-American, half Thai) and its sociological implications. An excerpt from an article written the following day by *Philadelphia Inquirer* sports columnist Bill Lyon poignantly summarized the significance of the occasion:

> Tiger Woods won a tournament of great prestige in one of the most exclusive and restrictive enclaves in the world, a place that, until recent years, he could have gained admission to only by way of the servant's entrance.
>
> The green-coated autocrats of Augusta National would have permitted him to clean their ashtrays and shine their shoes and serve them assorted beverages. But the only way he would have set a shoe onto those lush and fragrant fairways was as a caddy.
>
> Last night, in the gentle Georgia gloaming, those very same men stood to applaud as Tiger Woods slipped into a coat of the very same hue as theirs. They shook the hand of a 21-year-old prodigy, and their grip was sincere. The optimist in you would like to think that at that moment, we edged another inch up the progress chart.
>
> It will be recorded that, two days before the 50th anniversary of Jackie Robinson first playing in a Major League Baseball game, Woods became the first African American to win a Masters or, indeed, any major golf tournament.
>
> But this is too narrow, too constricting. Because through Tiger Woods courses the blood of five nationalities—not only African-American, but Chinese, Cherokee, Thai, and Dutch. Tiger Woods is a melting pot with a wedge.
>
> Better, then, that we celebrate him, and this, for what they are—a triumph for all humankind.

25 points, defeated the Liberty, 65–51, to capture the first WNBA title.

The Fall of Tyson, Part II

By the time he stepped into the boxing ring against Evander Holyfield on June 28, Mike Tyson had experienced a wild range of highs and lows, in and out of boxing. Right from the start of his professional career in 1985, Tyson's power-punching, street-fighting style intimidated opponents. He won 14 fights that year, 11 by first-round knockouts. A year later, "Iron Mike" won the World Boxing Council (WBC) heavyweight title, becoming the youngest heavyweight fighter, at age 20, to win a world title. By the end of 1987 he held the WBC, World Boxing Association (WBA), and International Boxing Federation (IBF) titles, making him the undisputed heavyweight champion.

In the meantime, his personal life took a beating. A brief and turbulent marriage to actress Robin Givens ended in divorce. In 1992, two years after his shocking loss to relative unknown Buster Douglas, he was convicted of raping an 18-year-old woman and served three years in prison. Tyson regained his WBC and WBA titles in 1996, but then lost the WBA title in November to Holyfield. Now came the rematch, which turned into one of sports' more bizarre spectacles.

The arena at the MGM Grand Garden in Las Vegas was packed for the greatly anticipated fight. Holyfield won the first two rounds on all three judges' scorecards. As Tyson prepared to come out for the third round, Holyfield pointed out that he'd forgotten his mouthpiece. Once the fight resumed, Tyson spit out the mouthpiece, grabbed Holyfield, and bit his right ear. The action had to be halted for four minutes while the ringside doctor tended to Holyfield's bleeding ear. But after the fight started up again, Tyson did the same thing, except this time he bit Holyfield's left ear.

Referee Mills Lane immediately stopped the fight and disqualified Tyson. While Holyfield went to the hospital for treatment, Tyson defended his actions, charging that Holyfield had illegally head-butted him in the first and second rounds. State boxing officials suspended Tyson and withheld his $30 million fee for the fight, pending an inquiry.

On July 9, the Nevada Athletic Commission revoked Tyson's boxing license for one year and fined him $3 million—which meant he ended up making $27 million. Tyson's Nevada boxing license was restored October 19, 1998, and he was back in the ring by January of the following year.

Legends Retire

Two nationally known college coaching legends decided to step down after long and storied careers at their schools. First, basketball's Dean Smith (b.1931) retired on October 9; then, on November 29, it was football's Eddie Robinson (1919–2007).

Smith was the head coach of the University of North Carolina Tar Heels for 36 years beginning with the 1961–62 season. He led his teams to two national championships, 17 Atlantic Coast Conference

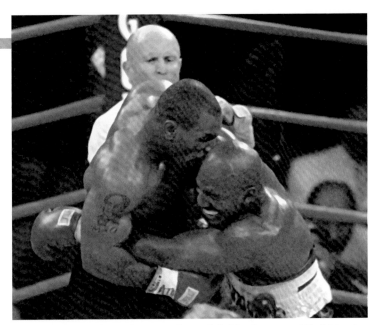

Reality Bites *Champion Evander Holyfield grimaces while bitten by challenger Mike Tyson in their heavyweight title fight. Tyson was fined and suspended, but soon was back in the boxing ring.*

titles, and 879 wins in all (a college record that stood until Bob Knight surpassed it in 2007). Twenty-seven of Smith's teams played in the NCAA tournament, including the last 23 in a row. His final team went 28–7 and advanced to the NCAA Final Four.

What Smith was to North Carolina basketball, Robinson was to the Grambling State University Tigers football team. Robinson was the head coach at the predominantly African-American school in Louisiana since 1941. He won 408 games (a record for any NCAA Division I coach) and led his teams to three perfect seasons and eight black national championships.

Both coaches sent dozens of players on to the professional ranks, but both also were equally intent on helping their players graduate.

More Unruly Behavior

Mike Tyson wasn't the only sports personality who couldn't control himself this year:

- In game five of the NBA Eastern Conference semifinals on May 14 in Miami, players from the New York Knicks and Miami Heat got into a bench-clearing brawl. The league suspended the Heat's P. J. Brown and the Knicks' Patrick Ewing, Charlie Ward, and Allan Houston for game six; Brown and the Knicks' Larry Johnson and John Starks were suspended for game seven. The Knicks, up three games to one entering game five, lost that game and the series.

- On September 25, veteran sportscaster Marv Albert pleaded guilty to misdemeanor assault and battery charges. It was revealed during the trial in Virginia that Albert had bitten his female accuser during sex. Hours after the verdict, he was fired from his announcer's job at NBC Sports and resigned as an announcer for the Madison Square Garden Network.

- Latrell Sprewell (b.1970), a guard for basketball's Golden State Warriors, punched and choked his head coach, P.J. Carlesimo, during practice on December 1. Sprewell claimed that he was provoked by ongoing verbal abuse from Carlesimo. In one of the most costly punishments in sports history, the NBA suspended Sprewell for one year and the Warriors terminated the remaining three years of his four-year, $32 million contract.

The One-Year Wonders

By winning the 1997 World Series, team owner H. Wayne Huizenga and his Florida Marlins proved that baseball in the 1990s had unmistakably become a game in which money talks. Following the 1995 season, which the Marlins finished with a record of 67–76, Huizenga devised a two-year upgrade plan. The owner of Blockbuster Video stores opened up his ample wallet to sign top pitchers Kevin Brown and Al Leiter in 1996 and Alex Fernandez in 1997. He bulked up the offense by adding Moises Alou, Darren Daulton, and Bobby Bonilla to the 1997 roster. The critical move, though, was hiring manager Jim Leyland, a proven winner who had navigated the Pittsburgh Pirates to three consecutive National League East titles from 1990 to 1992. Coupled with other complimentary acquisitions and its budding homegrown talent, Florida was poised to make a pennant run this year.

Behind strong pitching, Florida won a team-best 92 games during the regular season. That was second in the N.L. East to the 101–61 Atlanta Braves, but enough to qualify as the N.L. wildcard entry in the playoffs. The Marlins swept the San Francisco Giants in three games in the division series, then surprised the mighty Braves by taking the N.L. Championship Series (NLCS), four games to two in September.

The Cleveland Indians won the American League pennant with a power-packed lineup. Sluggers Jim Thome, Matt Williams, David Justice, Manny Ramirez, and Sandy Alomar Jr. led an offense that produced enough runs to overpower a mediocre pitching staff. Cleveland won the A.L. Central with an 86–75 record, knocked off the New York Yankees in the divisional series, and beat the Baltimore Orioles in six games in the ALCS.

The World Series came down to a thrilling seventh game on October 26 in Miami. In the bottom of the 11th inning, with the score tied 2–2, Florida shortstop Edgar Renteria hit a two-out, bases-loaded single off Charles Nagy to score Greg

Counsell. Thus the Marlins, in just their fifth season, became the quickest expansion team to win the World Series.

Baseball-wise, Huizenga's investments paid major dividends. Financially, however, the owner complained that he'd lost $30 million and wanted to sell the team. Ironically, to make the sale more attractive—that is, to lower the price of the team—he began unloading players within weeks after the Series. On Opening Day of 1998, an almost entirely new team took the field, leaving dismayed fans with only fleeting memories of glory. The Marlins went on the finish with the worst record in baseball, at 54–108. The following January, the team was sold.

Other Milestones of 1997

✔ Quarterback Danny Wuerffel, the 1996 Heisman Trophy winner, led the University of Florida to its first Division I college football national title following the school's 52–20 trouncing of rival Florida State University in the Sugar Bowl on January 2.

✔ The University of Tennessee's Lady Vols, paced by Chamique Holdsclaw's 24 points, topped Old Dominion University, 68–59, on March 30 to repeat as college basketball national champions.

✔ On June 13, the Chicago Bulls won their fifth NBA title of the 1990s. They beat the Utah Jazz, 90–86, in Chicago to take the series, 4–2. Michael Jordan was the MVP, averaging 32.3 points per game.

✔ On June 30, the Texas Rangers' Bobby Witt hit a home run in an interleague game against the Los Angeles Dodgers. What's so unusual about that? Well, Witt was the first American League pitcher since 1972 to hit a homer.

University of Tennessee

✔ On December 13, University of Michigan cornerback Charles Woodson became the first primarily defensive player to win the Heisman Trophy, awarded to college football's best player. Woodson would become the fourth player picked (by the Oakland Raiders) in the NFL draft in the spring of 1998, and would make the Pro Bowl in his first season in the league.

1998

Broncos Kick It Up

Terrell Davis scored a record three rushing touchdowns, including a one-yard run with 1:45 remaining, to lift the Denver Broncos past the Green Bay Packers 31–24 in Super Bowl XXXII on January 25 at San Diego's Qualcomm Stadium. Denver's victory was its first after four losses in as many Super Bowl appearances (dating to the 1977 season), and was the first for an AFC team in the Super Bowl since the 1983 season.

Three of the Broncos' four Super Bowl losses came with John Elway (b.1960) at quarterback. In his fourth try, the 37-year-old Elway at long last had a Vince Lombardi trophy and a championship ring—the missing pieces to go along with reams of spectacular statistics amassed over his 16 NFL seasons.

Elway only needed to be efficient against Green Bay (he passed for 123 yards and ran for a touchdown), thanks to Davis and an offensive line that could make a hole in anything. The AFC's top rusher that season (1,750 yards), Davis tortured the Packers' defense, gaining 157 yards on 30 carries and earning game MVP honors.

New Winter Games

From February 7 to 22, the modest mountain city of Nagano, Japan, a little more than an hour northwest of Tokyo, hosted 2,302 athletes from 72 countries as they participated in 68 events in the Winter Olympic Games. Among them were, for the first time as official medal sports, snowboarding, curling, and women's ice hockey. The United States won 13 medals at Nagano: six gold, three silver, and four bronze.

The super-fast Super G (giant slalom) course at the Hakuba downhill skiing venue provided one of the most golden moments of the Games for the United States. That's where Picabo Street turned previous tragedies into triumph. Only 14 months earlier, Street had crashed while training in Vail, Colorado, damaging ligaments, cartilage, and bone in her left knee. She recovered from reconstructive surgery in remarkable time, and began training for Nagano just before Thanksgiving 1997. Then, 11 days before the Olympics began, Street fell on a slope in Sweden and was knocked unconscious.

Her first of two events in Japan was the downhill, in which she took the silver

Curtain Call *Fans at St. Louis' Busch Stadium salute Mark McGwire, the new single-season home-run king (page 80).*

medal at the 1994 Games in Lillehammer, Norway. Though Street finished sixth in the downhill at Nagano, she kept her hopes high for the upcoming Super G.

Wearing a skintight, blazing yellow suit and racing on longer downhill skis, Street had a slight misstep about halfway through her final run, but recovered nicely. Her time of 1:18.02 put her in first place,

though her toughest competitors had yet to ski. Austria's Michaela Dorfmeister crossed the finish line at 1:18.03—giving Street the gold by a scant one one-hundredth of a second, the slimmest margin of victory possible.

Meanwhile, in the figure skating hall, 15-year-old Tara Lipinski skated her short program to a song from the movie *Anas-*

Upside Down *The 1998 Winter Olympics in Nagano, Japan, were host to a number of new medal sports. Among them: the extreme sport of snowboarding, a staple of the X Games.*

nament, which came down to a face-off between the United States and Canada. Throughout the 1990s the Canadians had dominated the sport, especially against the Americans, beating them in four world championships. Canada was fully expected to maintain its mastery in Nagano. But the United States won, 3–1, with clean, hard skating, solid goaltending, and timely goals.

Back on the ski slopes, the United States took three of the four gold medals in freestyle skiing. Eric Bergoust and Nikki Stone won the men's and women's aerials, respectively. Bergoust, with his gravity-defying aerobatics, set a world record with a pair of nearly perfect quadruple twisting triple flips. Stone nailed both her back somersaults to top the 12-woman field. Jonny Moseley, a free-spirited Californian, won the freestyle moguls event on the strength of his trademark helicopter jump—a 360-degree spin in the air while grabbing one of his crossed skis, followed by a pinpoint landing.

Birth of the BCS

It's not often easy breaking with tradition. And in the case of college football's system of bowl games, that tradition has roots that date back more than 100 years. Add to that the millions of dollars in payouts offered by the major traditional postseason bowl games, and the increasing calls for a college football playoff to determine the national champion have gone unheeded.

Nevertheless, the bowl format did undergo tinkering in 1998 in an attempt to decide a true national champion. Pre-

tasia. She did well, but her favored rival, fellow American Michelle Kwan (b.1980), skated slightly better and was in first place going into the decisive long program two nights later. Kwan went first among the six finalists and turned in what appeared to be a winning performance. But Lipinski skated a nearly flawless program. Her squeals of joy, as her scores come up indicating she'd captured the gold medal, echoed throughout the arena.

A lot of women took to the ice for the first Olympic women's hockey tourviously, the "champion" was declared by rival polls taken among sportswriters and coaches. Occasionally, those polls disagreed about the national champion, leading to endless debates.

In 1998, in the latest scheme to pair the No. 1 and No. 2 teams in the land in a single "championship" game, officials from the Orange, Sugar, Rose, and Fiesta bowls joined with the Atlantic Coast, Big East, Big 12, Big Ten, Pacific-10, and Southeastern conferences and the University of Notre Dame to form the Bowl Championship Series (BCS). A complex system, using national polls, computer tabulations, and strength of schedules, ranks teams and ultimately determines the bowl match-ups. (The formula has been tweaked several times since the original.) And in the decade-plus existence of the BCS, sometimes it has worked—and sometimes it has only led to more debate.

Beísbol in America

The Hispanic presence in Major League Baseball had been quietly growing since the 1970s. A small handful of players had appeared before that, most notably Hall of Famer Roberto Clemente (1934–1972) from Puerto Rico. In the 1990s, however, their numbers multiplied. In 1998, for instance, for the first time, the MVPs of both leagues were born in Latin American countries: for the National League, Sammy Sosa from the Dominican Republic; for the American League, Puerto Rico native Juan Gonzalez.

From 1990 to 2001, according to Northeastern University's Center for the Study of Sport in Society director, Peter Roby, the number of Hispanic major leaguers swelled to 26 percent from 13 percent; most were born outside the U.S. In the same period, the number of African Americans on Major League Baseball rosters declined to 13 percent from 17 percent and the percentage of white players shrank to 59 from 70. This reflected similar trends in the general U.S. population.

Dating back to the 1860s, baseball has a long and rich tradition in Cuba, the Dominican Republic, Puerto Rico, and other Latin American nations. Some Major League baseball teams used to have spring training camps and play exhibition games there. But not until about the same time Jackie Robinson broke the game's color barrier in 1947, did foreign-born Hispanics catch scouts' eyes. Over the coming decades, some would shine as among baseball's best, including Hall of Famers Juan Marichal (Dominican Republic), Rod Carew (Panama), Orlando Cepeda (Puerto Rico), Tony Perez (Cuba), and Luis Tiant (Cuba).

Hispanics continued to thrive, if not in numbers, then in stature, until the 1990s. That's when economics led to an influx of talented Latin players who could be signed for less money than what U.S. high school and college prospects commanded. By the end of the decade, virtually every major league franchise had opened baseball academies in the Dominican Republic, by far the region's greatest pool of talent. Besides Sosa, the island nation had by then produced such marquee names as Pedro Martinez, Manny Ramirez, Miguel Tejada, Raul Mondesi, and Jose Rijo.

1998

Hispanics on the 1998 All-Star teams included Sosa, Gonzalez, Alex Rodriguez, Ivan Rodriguez, brothers Roberto and Sandy Alomar, Moises Alou, Andres Galarraga, Javy Lopez, and Edgar Renteria. Second baseman Roberto Alomar—on the strength of his home run, walk, stolen base, and superb defensive play—won the MVP Award for the '98 All-Star game, which the A.L. won, 13–8.

Big E for Endurance

NASCAR could not have planned a more perfect beginning for its 50th anniversary season, as the sport's most popular driver won its most prestigious event—finally.

Long Time Coming *Legendary Dale Earnhardt (in the number-3 car) won the biggest race on the NASCAR circuit, the Daytona 500, for the first time on his 20th try.*

After 19 hope-filled tries and 19 frustrating failures, Dale Earnhardt succeeded in taking the checkered flag at the Daytona 500. "The Intimidator," as the hard-driving, highly competitive Earnhardt was known, already had seven Winston Cup driving championships, 70 career Cup wins, and 575 Cup starts under his seatbelt, including 30 on the hallowed, high-banked oval track at Daytona, Florida.

Earnhardt was 46 years old when he climbed into his famous black No. 3 Chevy on February 15, 1998. Since becoming NASCAR's Winston Cup Rookie of the Year in 1979, he had won just about every other race, but was on the brink of becoming one of those sports legends who never wins The Big One.

Earnhardt had been oh-so-close to winning Daytona before. Four times he'd lost the lead with 10 laps to go. He'd come up short twice on the last lap. This year, he had a pack of pesky pursuers on his tail as the 200-lap race neared its exciting conclusion. He held them all off, though, and a long-awaited celebration erupted. To conclude his most memorable victory lap, Earnhardt cruised down pit road (the stretch alongside a racetrack where pit crews are stationed), as drivers and crew members from virtually every team lined up to shake his hand. Then he went into the infield and did a couple of celebratory donuts (spinning his car in circles).

"I wish every race driver that ever runs Daytona could feel what we felt yesterday in Victory Lane," Earnhardt told reporters the following day. "That's one of the greatest feelings in your life, to work that many years and come so close and be so dominant and finally win that race."

The Man in Black

There was little doubt, when he was growing up in tiny Kannapolis, North Carolina, that Dale Earnhardt would some day race cars for a living. His father, Ralph Earnhardt, was one of stock car racing's pioneers during the 1950s, and young Dale soaked up the rough-and-tumble lifestyle. "I wanted to race—that's all I ever wanted to do," he once said. "I didn't care about work or school or anything. All I wanted to do was to work on race cars and then drive race cars. It was always my dream, and I was just fortunate enough to be able to live out that dream."

True to his word, Earnhardt quit school when he was 16 and made his Winston Cup debut in 1975, finishing 22nd in the World 600 at the Charlotte Motor Speedway in North Carolina. He joined NASCAR's "major league" circuit full-time in 1979. Earnhardt took his first Winston Cup win that season at Bristol Motor Speedway in Bristol, Tennessee, and was named Rookie of the Year. A year later, he became the first Winston Cup driver to win Rookie of the Year and Driver of the Year in successive seasons.

Along with six more championships, he claimed victory in nearly every major event on the circuit, including a career-best 11 wins in 1987. In 2000, when some wondered if he'd passed his prime, Earnhardt posted two wins, 13 top five finishes, and 24 top 10s, and came in second behind Jeff Gordon in the final points standings.

On February 18, 2001, Earnhardt started his 23rd Daytona 500 from the seventh position and was racing for third during the last lap. He had himself in position so that his teammate, Michael Waltrip, and his son, Dale Earnhardt Jr., would finish first and second, respectively. Suddenly, Dale Sr.'s No. 3 Chevy was bumped by another car, causing Earnhardt to crash head-on into the wall. He was killed instantly.

Wrote *AutoWeek* managing editor Roger Hart in tribute, "As we found out February 18 at the Daytona International Speedway, even being the best of the best—and make no mistake about it, Dale Earnhardt was the best stock car driver ever—is not always enough. Like many other race fans across the country, I will miss Dale Earnhardt. NASCAR racing will not be the same. He helped make stock car racing what it is today, and if there's any solace in his passing, it's that he loved every minute of it."

Lady Vols, Take Three

Women's sports flourished during the 1990s. From Little League to the Olympics, female athletes participated in ever-increasing numbers at higher and higher levels of competition. The highest profile sport for women was college basketball, which ran a fast break through the decade. And by winning their third straight NCAA national championship on March 29 at Kemper Arena in Kansas City, Missouri, the University of Tennessee's Lady Vols exemplified just how far the sport had advanced.

Coached by the celebrated Pat Summitt, in her 24th year at Tennessee, the Lady Vols steamrolled through the regular season undefeated, 33–0. They utterly dominated opponents, outscoring teams by an average margin of 30.1 points per game.

Chamique Holdsclaw, the junior forward and national player of the year, solidified her reputation as perhaps the best female college player ever. "Her

Little Guys Pound Big Homers

In a slugfest that would make Mark McGwire and Sammy Sosa proud, the Little League team from Toms River, New Jersey, out-homered the squad from Kashima, Japan, to win the Little League World Series, 12–9, on August 29 in Williamsport, Pennsylvania. This was the first American team to claim the title since Long Beach, California, won back-to-back championships in 1992 and 1993.

A total of 11 homers highlighted the game, six of them for the New Jersey team. Shortstop Chris Cardone hit a pair in consecutive at-bats—the second one a game-deciding two-run shot in the sixth inning. Tetsuya Furukawa belted three of Kashima's five home runs.

Besides several lead changes, the spirited international contest featured Sayaka Tsushima, the sixth girl to play in a Little League World Series, the first in a final, and the first from a Far East champion. She went 0 for 3.

Airness"—as she had become known, borrowing a nickname from Michael Jordan—not only averaged 23.5 points per game (including six NCAA tournament appearances), but demonstrated tremendous leadership to a pair of talented, but raw freshmen, Tamika Catchings and Semeka Randall.

The tournament's field of 64 teams showcased the burgeoning talent found at schools nationwide, but Tennessee was clearly at the head of the class. Its only speedbump along the road to Kansas City came in the Mideast Regional final versus the University of North Carolina, in which the Vols valiantly overcame a 12-point second-half deficit to prevail, 76–70. They played a near-perfect championship game, easily dispensing with Louisiana Tech University, 93–75. Holdsclaw—with 25 points, 10 rebounds, and six assists in the finale—was voted the Final Four's Most Outstanding Player.

Tennessee thus became the first women's team to claim three straight titles, and it was their sixth in 12 years.

"The best team doesn't always win," said Summitt in the post-game press conference, "but tonight, I thought the best team won a championship that they deserved."

Chasing 61

In 1998, the New York Yankees forged one of baseball's best seasons ever. The Bronx Bombers won 114 of 162 regular-season games, breezed through the American League playoffs, and then swept the National League-champion San Diego Padres in four games in the World Series. It was the Yankees' record 24th world championship.

Even still, the most memorable story line of the 1998 season had nothing to do with the Yankees. Instead, it was an epic battle for baseball's single-season home-run record. That chase, waged all summer long between the St. Louis Cardinals' Mark McGwire (b.1963) and the Chicago Cubs' Sammy Sosa (b.1968), captivated the nation, and helped win over the hearts of some fans who felt jilted during the 1994 players' strike.

McGwire smacked 11 homers by the end of April. Sosa had just six home runs by May 1, but went crazy in June, smacking a major league-record 20. At the All-Star break in July, Sosa had 33 home runs to McGwire's 37. The big-league record of 61 home runs by the Yankees (set in 1961) was in sight.

Sosa reached the 50 plateau on August 11; McGwire arrived there on the 20th. By the end of the month, when they both stood at 55 homers, Maris' widow and family were graciously and anxiously awaiting baseball history. They sat proudly in box seats at St. Louis' Busch Stadium on September 7 when McGwire tied the record at 61, and were back there the next day when he hit No. 62. Ironically, the record breaker was his shortest home run of the season.

On September 11, at Wrigley Field, Sosa kept pace with homers 61 and 62. He ended up hitting four more to finish at 66, while McGwire kept up his assault on the record books right up until the last day of the season, blasting two to finish with a phenomenal total of 70 home runs.

Other Milestones of 1998

✔ New Year's Day saw the University of Michigan end a 12–0 season with a 21–16 win over Washington State University in the Rose Bowl. Nonetheless, the Michigan Wolverines shared the number one college football ranking with 13–0 University of Nebraska.

✔ In January, CBS, Fox, and ABC/ESPN committed $17.6 billion from 1998 to 2005 to televise NFL games. Color analyst John Madden signed a five-year deal with Fox worth $8 million per year.

✔ A federal magistrate ruled, on February 11, that under the Americans with Disabilities Act, handicapped pro golfer Casey Martin could use a motorized golf cart in PGA tournaments, despite tournament rules to the contrary.

✔ A couple of baseball pitching gems: On May 6 in Chicago, 20-year-old Cubs rookie Kerry Wood tied

Ila Borders

a Major League record by striking out 20 Houston Astros in a 2–0 victory in his fifth career start. On May 17 at Yankee Stadium, veteran left-hander David Wells pitched the 15th perfect game ever (27 batters up, and 27 batters down) in a 4–0 win over Minnesota.

✔ In a labor dispute, NBA team owners imposed a player lockout on June 29 that would eventually shorten the 1998–1999 basketball season.

✔ On July 9, Ila Borders became the first female pitcher to start a minor league game. The 24-year-old lefty pitched five innings for the Duluth-Superior Dukes in their 8–3 loss to the Sioux Falls Canaries in the Northern League.

✔ Baltimore Orioles shortstop Cal Ripken ended his streak of consecutive games played at 2,632 on September 20 at Camden Yards. Ripken took himself out of the lineup.

1999

Elway Out on Top

Only one NFL player ever was named the Super Bowl MVP in the last game of his career. That player was quarterback John Elway, who guided the Denver Broncos to a 34–19 victory over the Atlanta Falcons in Super Bowl XXXIII at Pro Player Stadium in Miami on January 31.

It was the second consecutive Super Bowl victory for Elway and the Broncos, who beat the Green Bay Packers in game XXXII the previous January (see page 74). Before that, both Denver and its quarterback struggled to overcome the reputation that they couldn't win the Big One. The Broncos had lost the Super Bowl four times, three of them with Elway at quarterback. "You wonder," Elway once said, "if you run out of years."

Elway didn't run out of years, and got to retire on his own terms: after winning a Super Bowl. Against Atlanta, he completed 18 of 29 passes for 336 yards. Early in the fourth quarter, he ran 3 yards for the touchdown that helped put the game out of reach at 31–6. Soon afterward, he was holding aloft the Vince Lombardi Trophy in the Broncos' postgame celebration.

Money Players

On January 6, the Baseball Writers' Association of America (BBWAA) elected three first-time candidates into the National Baseball Hall of Fame in Cooperstown, New York: Nolan Ryan, George Brett, and Robin Yount (players are eligible for induction five years after they retire). The last time that happened was in 1936, and those players—Ty Cobb, Walter Johnson, Christy Mathewson, Babe Ruth, and Honus Wagner—were in the very first group of baseball players enshrined in the Hall of Fame.

The news brought cheers from baseball fans who appreciated the remarkable achievements of each player, although it particularly heartened sports collectors. For as much as money drove athletes, team owners, television networks, and corporate sponsors during the 1990s, the memorabilia and collectibles industry shifted into high gear during the decade, too. Values of trading cards and autographed items—from game-used jerseys to cancelled paychecks—skyrocketed.

The financial significance of the Hall of Fame announcement was the instant increase in price of items related to Ryan,

World Class *The United States hosted—and won—soccer's Women's World Cup (see page 86).*

Brett, and Yount. Getting into the Hall raises a player's stature, and therefore the worth of his likeness and things connected to him. For example, Ryan's rookie card (1968 Topps #177) rose from about $1,000 to nearly $3,000, practically overnight.

Proof of just how crazy the market had gotten surfaced on January 12, when the baseball that Mark McGwire hit for his historic 70th home run in 1998 sold at auction for slightly more than $3 million. A couple of weeks later, the buyer revealed himself: Todd McFarlane, the creator of *Spawn* and other superhero comic books and toys. In fact, the owner

of the so-called McFarlane Collection had plunked down another $300,000 or so to acquire McGwire's No. 1, 63, 67, 68, and 69 home-run balls, along with Sammy Sosa's No. 33, 61, and 66.

While you chew on that, consider Karen Shemonsky of Clarks Summit, Pennsylvania, who paid $7,475 for Cobb's false teeth—honestly—at a Sotheby's baseball memorabilia auction on September 27. "[Friends] keep calling me, saying, 'Why would you want that?'" Shemonsky told reporters. "My sister goes on cruises. I'd rather have this in my hand." Biting commentary on the times, for sure.

Two Out of Three Ain't Bad *Jockey Chris Antley rode Charismatic (6) to victory in the Kentucky Derby and the Preakness Stakes, but fell short of the coveted Triple Crown in the Belmont Stakes.*

Every Dog Has His Day

In the 1990s, the University of Connecticut Huskies were heralded from Juneau to Jupiter (Florida) for their outstanding basketball. UConn's men's program, since the arrival in 1986 of head coach Jim Calhoun, rose from the doghouse to the penthouse in the Big East Conference. And coach Geno Auriemma, guided the Lady Huskies to national prominence with a perfect season and a national championship in 1995.

It took four years for Calhoun's men to catch up, but they finally won it all in 1999, downing Duke University in the NCAA championship game, 77–74, on March 29 at Tropicana Field in St. Petersburg, Florida. Coming into the tournament, UConn held the unenviable record for most NCAA appearances (20) without reaching the Final Four. What made this championship even sweeter was vanquishing the Blue Devils, who had become UConn's nemesis in recent years. Seven times during the 1990s, UConn had played into the Sweet 16, and each time they'd fallen short—twice to Duke. The most devastating defeat was in the 1990 tournament, when Christian Laettner's last-second shot sent UConn home.

Duke, with only one loss all season and an immaculate 16–0 record in the tough Atlantic Coast Conference, was heavily favored. Yet UConn, with a 28–2 regular-season record, didn't exactly fit the underdog profile. Sure enough, coach Mike Krzyzewski's Blue Devils, powered by 6-foot-8, 260-pound forward Elton Brand—the national player of the year—couldn't stop the sharp shooting of UConn guard Richard "Rip" Hamilton, who went on a game-high 27-point tear. Shortly after Duke's Trajan Langdon was called for traveling while driving to score the potential game-winning basket, the Huskies fell into a celebratory dog pile on the court.

Charismatic, Not Charmed

For the third year in a row, a horse entered the Belmont Stakes with a chance to win thoroughbred racing's Triple Crown. And for the third year in a row, that horse fell short. This year, it was Charismatic that won the Kentucky Derby and the Preakness Stakes before finishing third in the Belmont on June 5 in New York. (In 1997, Silver Charm won the first two legs of the Triple Crown, and in 1998 Real Quiet did it. Through 2009, no horse has won the Triple Crown since Affirmed in 1978.)

After winning the Kentucky Derby at Churchill Downs in Louisville on May 1 and the Preakness Stakes two weeks later at Pimlico Race Course in Baltimore, Charismatic came out of the gate fast and strong at the Belmont. He remained in the lead until about an eighth of a mile was left on the mile-and-a-half racetrack, when a longshot, Lemon Drop Kid, passed him. Vision and Verse, another longshot, also overtook Charismatic.

In the race, Charismatic fractured two bones in his lower left foreleg (an area comparable to the human ankle). He had successful surgery the next day, but his racing days were over.

Won for the Good Guys

The NBA almost didn't happen this year. In the latest round of an ongoing struggle between owners seeking to control costs and players seeking to maximize their salaries, the first three months of the NBA season were cancelled. Without a contract between owners and players, owners locked out the players while negotiations went on between the two sides. The entire preseason and all games through mid-January were cancelled. Finally, to fans' relief, the season began on February 2.

The second edition of the Bulls-without-Jordan NBA Finals (after a shortened regular season of 50 games instead of 82) was a Good Guys versus Bad Guys showdown in June, pitting the angelic San Antonio Spurs against the devilish New York Knicks. The typecasting was a no-brainer, with gentle giants David Robinson and Tim Duncan set to slay New York's surly Marcus Camby and coach-choking Latrell Sprewell (see page 72).

In the end, the Spurs smote the Knicks in five games to gain their first championship in the team's 26-year history. The lopsided outcome, however, had more to do with New York's offensive ineptitude and inability to stop San Antonio's twin seven-foot towers than any clash of virtues. After the title-clincher in New York on June 25, in which Finals MVP Duncan scored 31 points in the 78–77 San Antonio victory, Spurs head coach Gregg Popovich told Knicks head coach Jeff Van Gundy, "I've got Tim and you don't. That's the difference."

When Dallas Froze Over

Until the 1990s, NHL teams had been located almost exclusively in cold-weather cities, with the exception of the Los Angeles Kings. Then ice-challenged places such as Miami, Atlanta, Phoenix, and Dallas landed teams. On June 19 at the Marine Midland Arena in Buffalo, the Dallas Stars—which relocated from Minneapolis, Minnesota, in 1993—became the first Sun Belt team to hoist the Stanley Cup.

It took some effort to lift it over their heads. In game six of the best-of-seven series, the Stars, up three games to two, played the Buffalo Sabres to a 1–1 tie in regulation and two overtime periods. At 14:51 of the third overtime, Dallas rightwinger Brett Hull scored the

1999

winning goal. Or did he? Replays seemed to show that his left skate was illegally in the goal crease before he shot, which would have voided the goal. Despite the Sabres' strong protest, NHL officials let it stand. It went down in the record books as the second-longest overtime game in the history of the Stanley Cup finals, the longest to decide a winner—and, unofficially, the most controversial.

U.S. on Top of the World

On July 10, a crowd of 90,185 at the Rose Bowl in Pasadena, California—the largest ever to watch a women's sporting event anywhere—witnessed the United States outduel China in a thrilling penalty-kick shootout to win the 1999 Women's World Cup soccer tournament. The shootout followed a 0–0 tie after 90 minutes of regulation play and a scoreless 30-minute overtime. United States defender Brandi Chastain blasted the winning shot past Chinese goalkeeper Gao Hong to break a 4–4 deadlock.

World Cup '99 drew record crowds over its three-week, seven-city tournament, held June 19 to July 10.

The American women steamrolled through the first round, outscoring their three opponents 13–1. In the quarterfinals, they outlasted Germany, 3–2, then shut out Brazil, 2–0, to advance to the finals against their archrivals.

The United States had beaten China in both the 1991 World Cup and the 1996 Olympic championship games. This final turned into a grueling stalemate. It boiled down to the final shootout, during which five players from each team

alternate shots on goal from 12 yards out. After China tied it at 3–3, American star Mia Hamm—goalless in her last four games—nailed a pressure-packed kick. China answered, and then came 30-year-old Chastain's date with soccer immortality. When the Rose Bowl exploded with cheers, Chastain dropped to her knees and pulled off one of the more memorable celebrations ever. She ripped off her jersey to reveal a sports bra. The image of Chastain excitedly ripping off her jersey, as the men have long done in soccer, became an icon for tough, exuberant female athletes all over the world.

That wasn't the end of this heroic championship squad. With national attention focused on them, the eight-team Women's United Soccer Association (WUSA) professional league was formed, and all 20 of the '99 Cup players signed on, along with a roster of premier international stars. WUSA launched on April 14, 2001, with Chastain's Bay Area CyberRays facing off against Hamm's Washington Freedom at Robert F. Kennedy Stadium in Washington, D.C. The Freedom defeated the CyberRays, 1–0.

All-Star All-Star Game

Major League Baseball's annual All-Star Game is traditionally a mid-season break, where the game's top players shine for a couple of innings apiece to the fans' delight. The 1999 edition, however, played under the lights on July 13 at Boston's vintage Fenway Park, turned into an especially lustrous affair.

Along with some sparkling individual performances, the sport itself put on a spectacular show. As the last All-Star Game of the 20th century, MLB used the occasion to announce the nominees for its All-Century Team in an emotional pre-game ceremony. Onto the diamond trotted such living legends as outfielders Hank Aaron, Stan Musial, and Willie Mays, pitchers Bob Feller, Juan Marichal, Bob Gibson, and Sandy Koufax, and catchers Johnny Bench and Yogi Berra.

The loudest ovation, however, was saved for Ted Williams (1918–2002). Williams played for Boston from 1939 to 1960 and retired in 1960 with 521 home runs and a career .344 average. He earned a reputation as the greatest hitter who ever lived. However, the gruff and un-compromising Hall of Famer actually had not always been a fan favorite during his playing days in Boston.

For this night, though, the 80-year-old Williams, known as "the Splendid Splinter," was universally beloved—by the capacity crowd of 34,187, his fellow All-Century candidates, and the game's all-stars. Two strokes and a broken hip in recent years forced Williams to take the field in a golf cart, which he rode around Fenway to thunderous applause. He climbed out near the pitcher's mound, and, after tossing the ceremonial first pitch, was spontaneously surrounded by players past and present. "There was a baseball love-in on the mound," wrote the Associated Press the next day. "The stars of the night and the stars of the century swamping Ted Williams, gazing at him in awe, reaching over each other to shake his hand."

The game got off to a sizzling start when hometown Red Sox pitcher Pedro

How Sweep It Is

Following the events at the All-Star Game, baseball fell into its predictable pattern. After winning their respective divisions, the New York Yankees and Atlanta Braves powered through two rounds of the playoffs to meet in the World Series, October 23 to 27. It was billed as a showdown to decide not just the best team of the year, but also of the decade. Although the Braves had only captured one World Series since 1990 (defeating the Cleveland Indians in 1997), compared to two for the Yankees (1996 versus Atlanta, 1998 versus the San Diego Padres), the Braves had dominated the National League, winning eight division titles and five league championships.

It didn't turn out to be much of a battle. But for a lone defeat at the right arm of eventual A.L. Cy Young Award winner Pedro Martinez in game three of the A.L. Championship Series, the Yankees went undefeated in the entire postseason, winning 11 of 12 games. In sweeping the Braves in four straight games, the Yankees starting pitchers only gave up seven earned runs and held opposing batters to a paltry .200 average. New York relief pitcher and Series MVP Mariano Rivera pitched 4 2/3 innings, earned two saves, and registered an unblemished earned run average of 0.00.

Martinez struck out all three batters in the first inning—an All-Star Game record. In the bottom of the first, the American League scored two runs off N.L. starter Curt Schilling. Then Martinez came back out and struck out two more batters in the second, including St. Louis' home run king, Mark McGwire. Martinez's two stellar innings earned him the game's Most Valuable Player award.

The Baltimore Orioles' Cal Ripken Jr. and a trio of Cleveland Indians (Kenny Lofton, Manny Ramirez, and Roberto Alomar) each drove in a run in the American League's 4–1 victory.

1999

It's About the Bike

Among the most grueling competitions in sports is the annual Tour de France bicycle race. Even for a world-class athlete in peak condition, biking 2,287 miles around France over 20 days may be the ultimate physical and mental challenge. Now imagine doing it after surviving a near-fatal bout with cancer.

Meet Lance Armstrong. By winning the 1999 Tour de France on July 25—for the first of an amazing seven times in a row—the 27-year-old Texan did more than conquer the brutal course and 179 of the world's top cyclists. He beat death. In October 1996, he was diagnosed with testicular cancer, which rapidly spread throughout his body, including to his lungs and brain. When asked to calculate Armstrong's

odds of survival, the doctor said candidly, "Almost none." After two operations to remove golf ball-sized tumors and extensive chemotherapy, Armstrong launched his courageous comeback early in 1998.

He had shown flashes of brilliance in his racing career, winning the one-day World Championship in 1993 and individual stages of the Tour in 1993 and 1995. Yet his poor showings in the Tour's exhausting mountain climbs had denied Armstrong the chance to join Greg Le-Mond as the only other American to win cycling's most prestigious event. This year, fueled by the same indomitable spirit it took to overcome his lethal disease, Armstrong annihilated the mountain stages.

Riding with the U.S. Postal Service team, Armstrong won the 86th Tour's opening sprint, which allowed him to begin the race wearing the overall leader's yellow jersey. He lost it, then regained it for good in the eighth stage. He attacked the Alps and Pyrenees with such undaunted strength that the French media wondered if he was using banned performance-enhancing drugs. Armstrong overcame those obstacles, too, when race officials cleared him of any wrongdoing.

By the start of the 20th and final stage, Armstrong held an insurmountable lead of 6:19 minutes over his closest competitor. Resplendent in the yellow jersey, he pedaled triumphantly down Paris' famed Champs Elysees to the finish line, 7:37 ahead of Switzerland's Alex Zuelle. Besides winning four stages, including the toughest of the long mountain stages, Armstrong claimed a victory for cancer survivors everywhere.

Sister, Sister *The Williams sisters (Serena, left, and Venus) became the dominant players in women's tennis at the turn of the century. They teamed to win the U.S. Open doubles title in 1999.*

Other Milestones of 1999

✔ The University of Tennessee won the Fiesta Bowl on January 4, beating Florida State University, 23–16, to gain its first national championship in 47 years. It was the first national title game played as part of the new Bowl Championship Series (see page 76), which took effect in the 1998 college season.

✔ On March 4 in San Jose, the top-ranked Purdue University women's basketball team defeated Duke, 62–45, to claim its first NCAA national title.

✔ At a track and field meet in Athens, Greece, on June 16, Maurice Greene ran the 100-meter sprint in a world record time of 9.79 seconds.

✔ New York Yankees pitcher David Cone recorded the 16th perfect game in Major League baseball history on July 18, shutting out the Montreal Expos, 6–0, at Yankee Stadium.

✔ On August 7, a day after baseball star Tony Gwynn of the San Diego Padres collected his 3,000th career hit, Wade Boggs, then with the Tampa Bay Devil Rays,

David Cone celebrates with Joe Girardi.

became the first to reach the mark with a home run (against the Cleveland Indians). It turned out to be the last homer of Boggs' 18-year career.

✔ CBS renewed its broadcast rights to the NCAA men's basketball tournament on November 18 by signing a $6-billion, 11-year contract.

Sister Act

While other fathers in his Los Angeles neighborhood were taking their daughters to birthday parties or ballet lessons, Richard Williams watched his two little girls hit tennis balls to each other. Venus (b.1980) and her sister Serena (b. 1981), younger by 15 months, began playing tennis at age four and entered their first tournament when they were nine and eight.

The Williams sisters were 18 and 17 in 1999. They'd both turned pro and had quickly risen in the Women's Tennis Association's world rankings. In September, at the U.S. Open in Flushing, New York, Serena ruled the day.

Seeded seventh in the tournament, she engineered several upsets en route to her first career Grand Slam singles title. Serena not only became the lowest seed to win the women's title in the Open Era (since 1968) but also the second African-American woman ever (after Althea Gibson [b. 1927]) to win a Grand Slam singles title. A day later, she and big sis captured the Open doubles title. The two went on to dominate women's tennis into the new millennium.

RESOURCES

1990s Events and Personalities

Bill Clinton (Presidential Leaders)
By Michael Benson (Minneapolis, Minnesota: Lerner Publications, 2003).
A profile of the one of the most charismatic, and controversial, presidents in United States history.

Legends in Sports: Michael Jordan
By Matt Christopher (New York: Little, Brown Books for Young Readers, 2008).
A look at the basketball superstar from one of the most well-known writers on sports for young readers.

Play Baseball the Ripken Way
By Cal Ripken Jr. and Bill Ripken, with Larry Burke (New York: Ballantine Books, 2005).
The baseball legend offers tips and insights in an illustrated guide to the fundamentals of the sport.

Venus and Serena Williams: A Biography
By Jacqueline Edmondson (Westport, Connecticut: Greenwood Press, 2005).
Part of the Greenwood Biographies Series, the author tells the life stories of tennis' most famous siblings.

American Sports History

The Complete Book of the Olympics
By David Wallechinsky and Jaime Loucky (London: Aurum Press, 2008)
An extremely detailed look at every Winter and Summer Olympics from 1896 to the present, including complete lists of medal winners and short biographies of important American and international athletes.

The Encyclopedia of North American Sports History, Second Edition
By Ralph Hickok (New York: Facts on File, 2002)
This title includes articles on the origins of all the major sports as well as capsule biographies of key figures.

Encyclopedia of Women and Sport in America
Edited by Carol Oglesby et al. (Phoenix: Oryx Press, 1998)
A large overview of not only key female personalities on and off the playing field, but a look at issues surrounding women and sports.

Encyclopedia of World Sport
Edited by David Levinson and Karen Christensen (New York: Oxford University Press, 1999)
This wide-ranging book contains short articles on an enormous variety of sports, personalities, events, and issues, most of which have some connection to American sports history. This is a great starting point for additional research.

The ESPN Baseball Encyclopedia

Edited by Gary Gillette and Pete Palmer (New York: Sterling, 2008, fifth edition)

This is the latest version of a long-running baseball record and stats books, including the career totals of every Major Leaguer. Essays in the book cover baseball history, team history, overviews of baseball in other countries, and articles about the role of women and minorities in the game.

ESPN SportsCentury

Edited by Michael McCambridge (New York: Hyperion, 1999)

Created to commemorate the 20th century in sports, this book features essays by well-known sportswriters as well as commentary by popular ESPN broadcasters. Each decade's chapter features an in-depth story about the key event of that time period.

NFL Record & Fact Book

Edited by Jon Zimmer, Randall Liu, and Matt Marini (New York: Time Inc. Home Entertainment, 2010)

An indispensable reference source for NFL fans and media personnel.

The Sporting News Chronicle of 20th Century Sports

By Ron Smith (New York: BDD/Mallard Press, 1992)

A good single-volume history of key sports events. They are presented as if written right after the event, thus giving the text a "you are there" feel.

Sports of the Times

By David Fischer and William Taafe. (New York: Times Books, 2003)

A unique format tracks the top sports events on each day of the calendar year. Find out the biggest event for every day from January 1 to December 31.

Sports History Web Sites

ESPN.com

www.sports.espn.go.com

The Web site run by the national cable sports channel contains numerous history sections within each sport. This one for baseball is the largest and includes constantly updated statistics on baseball.

Official League Web Sites

www.nfl.com
www.nba.com
www.mlb.com
www.nhl.com

Each of the major sports leagues has history sections on their official Web sites.

Official Olympics Web Site

http://www.olympic.org/uk/games/index_uk.asp

Complete history of the Olympic Games, presented by the International Olympic Committee.

The Sports Illustrated Vault

http://sportsillustrated.cnn.com/vault/

Since its first issue in 1954, Sports Illustrated *has been a must-read for fans everywhere. You can go down memory lane in this trove of features, photos, and covers from the magazine.*

Sports Reference

www.sports-reference.com

By far the most detailed central site, including separate sections on baseball, basketball, football, hockey, and the Olympics. The sections include player stats, team histories, records from all seasons past, and much more.

INDEX